Narita Bahra KC is one of the most sought after and able Defence Barristers in the UK. Instructed to defend in high profile and heavyweight Tier 1 Financial Crime, Serious Crime and Regulatory cases.

Narita's fearless and tenacious approach makes her widely sought after by professional and lay clients. She is recognised as a King's Counsel who can skilfully deal with the most difficult of cases. Her investigative approach results in leading her team to successful outcomes.

Nominated as Financial Crime Silk 2023

Winner of 'Women of Achievement Award' 2020

Winner of 'Criminal Lawyer 2019' Legal Awards 2019

Winner of 'Legal Excellence Awards' Signature Awards

Shortlisted for "Women in Law Award – 100 Years Legal Awards 2019

Narita is recognised as a specialist in Disclosure. Her instruction in numerous high-profile cases has resulted in disclosure failings by prosecuting authorities being unmasked.

Narita is recognised as a specialist in expert witness cases. Narita's first case in silk resulted in disqualification of an expert witness. Since that date many of Narita's expert witness cases have attracted substantial media coverage. Narita was then instructed in the ensuing special appeals at the Court of Appeal.

Narita is ranked as a Tier 1 Silk in Financial Crime. Her publication on Confiscation and Restraint has become a trusted practical guide for lawyers.

Narita appears as a legal correspondent and presenter on National TV and Radio

Narita is a regular contributor to legal journals.

Narita's success as a female Crime Silk who is smashing traditional stereotypes is recognised the legal profession and national media. Narita was the first King's Counsel to mark the centenary of women entering the legal profession.

Narita is Master of the Bench for The Honourable Society of Lincoln's Inn.

Don Ramble is a specialist prosecution barrister with over 20 years' experience in the criminal courts. He has acted as disclosure counsel in some of the highest profile criminal trials in recent years, establishing himself as an expert in the field. His reputation and knowledge sees him called upon regularly to advise on disclosure issues in some of the most serious and complicated of cases.

Don is also currently acting as Deputy First Junior Counsel to a long-running and complex public inquiry.

TACKLING DISCLOSURE IN THE CRIMINAL COURTS

A Practitioner's Guide

Second Edition Focusing on Digital Disclosure

TACKLING DISCLOSURE IN THE CRIMINAL COURTS

A Practitioner's Guide

Second Edition Focusing on Digital Disclosure

Narita Bahra KC

Barrister, 33 Chancery Lane

Don Ramble

Barrister, 5 St. Andrew's Hill

Law Brief Publishing

Published 2023 by Law Brief Publishing, an imprint of Law Brief Publishing Ltd
30 The Parks
Minehead
Somerset
TA24 8BT

www.lawbriefpublishing.com

Paperback: 978-1-916698-19-2

To Jonathan Coggins, a sagacious pupil master.

For DCMP, Jack and Leo.

FOREWORD TO THE SECOND EDITION

This is a simply invaluable book for criminal practitioners, most particularly in light of the rapidly changing disclosure landscape in England and Wales. When I was a pupil barrister 45 years ago, disclosure routinely consisted of no more than a few handwritten statements, usually from extraneous witnesses, provided at the beginning of a trial. In a similar vein, the leading authorities establishing the considerable prosecutorial responsibilities in this field and Part 1 of the Criminal Procedure and Investigations Act 1996, which provides the governing statutory regime, are from an age that had not experienced or anticipated the full impact of the explosion of digital material, now measured glibly in terabytes. Our present disclosure arrangements were conceived, therefore, in a world when the prosecution could be expected to have a real understanding of the materials in their possession, even if that sometimes involved a considerable amount of work in truly complicated cases. Now, in even the most routine prosecution, that is usually a wholly unrealistic expectation.

It is my view that this aspect of criminal proceedings needs urgent revisiting. Although the investigators will have seized the digital devices and in that sense bear a particular duty based on their access to them, otherwise I consider that the responsibility for interrogating any digital material should be couched explicitly as being shared jointly by the prosecution and the defence. If the prosecution are on notice of relevant lines of enquiry potentially helpful to the defendant that they can reasonably pursue, that should occur. I recognise that to a very real extent there has been significant movement in identifying the responsibilities of the accused in this context, as reflected in the numerous sources of guidance that have recently been issued, such as the July 2022 Attorney-General's Guidelines. But notwithstanding these changes, the prosecution is too frequently close to being overwhelmed by the large volume of digital material they have either seized or to which they have access on the cloud. With worrying frequency prosecutions are abandoned or convictions are overturned on appeal because of the extent of the difficulties, or perceived prosecutorial failings, in this process.

The reality is that only a small fraction of the available digital material will, or can be, considered in advance of a trial. This needs to be faced. Criminal trials, having been prepared sensibly, should provide finality. If the defence have failed to assist sufficiently in the interrogation of the digital information in advance of the trial, the later discovery of potentially useful material should by no means necessarily lead to the conviction being overturned. As with the approach to all "fresh evidence" on which an appellant seeks to rely before the Court of Appeal, there should be a careful enquiry as to why the defendant had failed to alert the prosecution authorities to the possible existence of the particular exculpatory material, which had not been sought prior to trial.

It is to be stressed that the defendant is expected to secure all the relevant witnesses in advance of his or her trial. The same, in my view, should apply to any digital material, regardless of the fact that access to it may be – certainly in the first instance – via the prosecution authorities. If the responsibility should correctly be framed as being jointly held by the prosecution and the defence, I suspect there will be a greater need for judicial involvement, from an early stage in the case, to ensure that both parties – equipped the necessary tools – have discharged their obligations in this regard.

It is my belief, therefore, that the concept of "disclosure", certainly in this digital context, is to a significant extent outdated, and the process should be recognised as constituting something else, more akin to concurrent lines of enquiry (with the prosecution always needing to investigate realistic avenues of defence of which they are on notice or should sensibly anticipate). If the defendant fails to participate in this exercise, there may well be consequences if he or she later complains that there has been material non-disclosure.

But these are merely the ruminations of an old judge! In the meantime, operating as we must within the present framework, this is the up-to-date edition of an invaluable guide which will give practitioners the best chance of navigating these uncertain seas, avoiding the squalls, submerged rocks and whirlpools that await the unalert. The authors are to be commended for an accessible, well written, scrupulously researched and finely balanced resource.

Lord Justice Fulford
(Sitting in Retirement)
16 August 2023

FOREWORD TO THE FIRST EDITION

Disclosure is central to fairness in our criminal justice system. Getting it right matters – to defendants, complainants and the public interest in criminal prosecutions. Miscarriages of justice, flowing from disclosure failures and resulting in loss of liberty, are obvious disasters. Conversely, disclosure must neither be perceived as, nor allowed to become, unduly burdensome, so derailing trials which should otherwise have proceeded to a conclusion – or acting as a deterrent to the prosecution of (electronically) document heavy cases, a socially corrosive outcome.

The law, contained in the *Criminal Procedure and Investigations Act 1996*, together with the applicable Rules and other guidance, is settled and straightforward. The application of the law has proved less so.

The right mindset is of the first importance; the exercise must be thought through and disclosure must never be a box-ticking exercise. So too, an investigative mindset is crucial; for example, investigations must not be skewed by mis-characterising complainants (entitled of course to respect, dignity and the protection of their own Human Rights) as victims in cases where the issue in dispute is whether any crime has been committed.

All concerned have a part to play in correctly applying the law on disclosure. As I suggested in my (2011) "*Review of Disclosure in Criminal Proceedings*":

> "*Improvements in disclosure must be prosecution led or driven, in such a manner as to require the defence to engage – and to permit the defence to do so with confidence. The entire process must be robustly case managed by the judiciary. The tools are available; they need to be used.*" (at para. 8(iii)).

A key current concern relates to problems of scale given the volume of digital material, routinely generated. Technology may be said to have created this problem and, I am confident, technology (very likely AI) will one day solve it – but not yet. In the meantime, it is right that much effort is devoted by the CPS, the police, the professions and the Judiciary to addressing disclosure problems through the *National Disclosure Plan*; improvements in disclosure are correctly seen as essential to public confidence in the criminal justice system.

Against this background, the authors, Narita Bahra QC and Don Ramble, are to be commended – for their clear definition of the nature of the disclosure problem and their practical approach to tackling it. Notably, the structure of the book is easy to follow; it is also comprehensive, dealing alike with disclosure in the magistrates' court and the Crown Court.

As is readily apparent, the authors speak with the real benefit of practical experience. *Tackling Disclosure in the Criminal Courts – A Practitioner's Guide*, is a most helpful addition to the literature in an area where the need for problem-solving is ever necessary.

Sir Peter Gross
September 2019

PREFACE

This book is intended to provide practical guidance when considering issues of disclosure in criminal proceedings. It is aimed at both prosecution and defence practitioners. Disclosure issues can arise in any criminal case and in many guises, from the prosecution seeking an adverse inference from the defendant's failure to set out his case in the defence statement, to the defence applying for proceedings to be stayed as an abuse of process due to disclosure failings by the prosecution.

In some of the chapters, we have included checklists designed to help the reader ask the right questions when considering particular disclosure topics and have also included a number of precedents, pro-formas and sample documents to assist.

In this new edition, we have focused and provided more guidance in relation to the best approach to tackling the ever-increasing quantities of digital material.

We have also considered the impact of the revised Attorney General's Guidelines on Disclosure, which came into effect on 25 July 2022 and, in the context of disclosure in cases involving expert evidence, the Criminal Practice Directions 2023, which came into force on 29 May 2023.

The law is believed to be correct at the time of writing; 1 June 2023.

Narita Bahra KC
Don Ramble
July 2023

TABLE OF CASES

CONTENTS

INTRODUCTION

"To say that disclosure is straightforward is both to tell the truth and to mislead."

– Richard Horwell KC, Mouncher Investigation Report

Broadly speaking, unused material consists of all the relevant material and information that the prosecution have in their possession, but which has not been served on the defence as evidence. The prosecution must review this material to ensure that they disclose to the defence anything which might reasonably be considered capable of undermining the prosecution case against a defendant or of assisting the case for the defence. If an item of unused material undermines or assists, then it must be disclosed to the defence.

Both the prosecution and defence have obligations in relation to unused material. The prosecution must, for example, provide the defence with a schedule setting out the unused material in its possession. The defence are under an obligation to set out what the issues are in the case in their defence statement so that the prosecution are in a position to determine whether there is anything that might assist them.

Chapter One provides the context for this book in the form of a brief history of disclosure law. From its early beginnings, reliant on prosecution counsel's duty to act fairly and at a time when there were few document-heavy cases, through miscarriages of justice and disclosure failings leading to increased guidance, legislation in the form of the *Criminal Procedure and Investigations Act* 1996, and numerous reviews.

Despite the history, disclosure failings continue to arise in the criminal courts in a digital age where even the most seemingly straightforward of cases can now generate vast quantities of data.

Chapter Two seeks to get to grips with the terminology. We set out the basics of what disclosure means, for example, what an MG6C schedule is and what "sensitive" and "non-relevant" material consists of.

In **Chapter Three** we consider in more detail the key concepts of "initial disclosure" and "continuing disclosure", which have replaced what was previously called "primary disclosure" and "secondary disclosure". We also review the principles that apply to post-trial disclosure.

Chapter Four reviews the service of defence statements and we provide some practical advice as to how these documents are best deployed. We also consider the importance of witness notices.

In **Chapter Five** we take a look at disclosure requests, from the viewpoint of using them as part of a defence case strategy but also from a prosecution perspective.

In **Chapter Six** we focus on disclosure issues that arise in the magistrates' court.

In **Chapter Seven** we consider the approach to take to cases involving digital material, including mobile phone data and social media content.

In **Chapter Eight** we consider some key point to bear in mind when conducting cases involving expert witnesses.

In **Chapter Nine** we examine the subject of third-party material and what steps can be taken to obtain documentation that is not in the possession of the prosecution. We also consider the proper approach to the redaction of documents.

Chapter Ten sets out the procedure applicable to PII applications and when they are appropriate.

In **Chapter Eleven** we look at practical steps that can be taken by the prosecution and the defence to avoid the common disclosure pitfalls that can arise.

Chapter Twelve sets out what we consider to be best practice of what to do when a disclosure problem does arise. Again, we look at the steps that can be taken from both the prosecution and defence perspectives. We have also provided a number of case studies. These are fictional cases which exemplify common themes in this book. We look at how best to tackle the disclosure problems raised in these sample cases.

In **Chapter Thirteen** we have set out some practical tips to ensure that you claim what you are entitled to under the appropriate costs rules.

CHAPTER ONE

DEVELOPMENT OF DISCLOSURE LAW

This chapter provides the context for the issues explored in the rest of the book. We trace the genesis of disclosure law from its early beginnings to the current regime.

Disclosure began as a relatively informal process, left to prosecution counsel's duty to act fairly. As was stated in the case of *R v Puddick* (1865) 4 F & F 497, "*...counsel for the prosecution...are to regard themselves as ministers of justice, not to struggle for a conviction....*".

R v Bryant and Dickson

One of the Court of Appeal's earliest pronouncements on the prosecution's disclosure duties, was in the case of *R v Bryant and Dickson* [1946] 31 Cr. App. R. 146, at 151:

> *"In the opinion of the Court, the duty of the prosecution in such a case is to make available to the defence a witness whom the prosecution know can, if he is called, give material evidence."*

Dallison v Caffrey

Two decades later, in *Dallison v Caffrey* [1965] 1 QB 348, Lord Denning MR stated, at page 369,

> *"The duty of a prosecuting counsel or solicitor, as I have always understood it, is this: if he knows of a credible witness who can speak to material facts which tend to show the prisoner to be innocent, he must either call that witness himself or make his statement available to the defence. It would be highly reprehensible to conceal from the court*

the evidence which such a witness can give. If the prosecuting counsel or solicitor knows, not of a credible witness, but a witness whom he does not accept as credible, he should tell the defence about him so that they can call him if they wish."

In the same case, Diplock LJ went on to state at pages 375-376 in relation to the prosecutor:

"If he happens to have information from a credible witness which is inconsistent with the guilt of the accused, or although not inconsistent with his guilt, is helpful to the accused, the prosecutor should make such witness available to the defence..."

The Attorney General's Guidelines 1981 and the definition of "unused material"

Over the years, the increase in the number of individuals within the prosecution team, combined with the volume of material generated in investigations, made it inevitable that the process of reviewing unused material would become more formalised.

In December 1981, the 'Attorney General's Guidelines: Disclosure of Information to the Defence in Cases to be Tried on Indictment' (1982) 74 Cr.App.R. were issued.

For the first time, these guidelines referred to the term, "unused material" which was described as referring to:

"(i) All witness statements and documents which are not included in the committal bundles served on the defence.

(ii) The statements of any witnesses who are to be called to give evidence at committal and (if not in the bundle) any documents referred to therein.

(iii) The unedited version(s) of any edited statements or composite statement included in the committal bundles."

The Guidelines provided that,

> *"In all cases which are due to be committed for trial, all unused material should normally...subject to the discretionary exceptions...be made available to the defence solicitor if it has some bearing on the offence(s) charged and the surrounding circumstances of the case."*

Interestingly, those *"discretionary exceptions"* included statements:

> *"believed to be wholly or partially untrue and might be of use in cross-examination if the witness should be called by the defence"* and statements, *"favourable to the prosecution and believed to be substantially true but there are grounds for fearing that the witness due to loyalty or fear, might give the defence solicitor a quite different, and false, story favourable to the defendant. If called as a defence witness upon the basis of this second account, the statement to the police can be of use in cross-examination."*

The prosecution were, therefore, given the discretion of deciding when disclosure should be made in accordance with these Guidelines. This discretion also included decisions not to disclose material if it was sensitive.

There then followed a series of Court of Appeal decisions, which allowed appeals based on failures in the disclosure process. The prosecution in these cases were criticised for the way in which they had exercised their discretion under the Attorney General's Guidelines. By far the most prominent of these authorities was the case of Judith Ward.

R v Ward

In September 1973, a bomb exploded at Euston railway station. Several people were injured but no one was killed. In February 1974, a bomb exploded in a coach carrying soldiers and their families along the M62 motorway. Twelve people were killed and many more were injured. A week later, at the National Defence College, another bomb exploded injuring many people.

In October 1974, Judith Ward was charged with three counts of causing explosions likely to endanger life or property relating to the bomb explosions at Euston, on the coach on the M62 and at the National Defence College, and with 12 counts of murder relating to each of the persons killed by the explosion on the coach.

At the trial, the prosecution relied upon confessions and admissions made by Miss Ward in interviews with the police, together with scientific evidence to the effect that traces of nitroglycerine had been found on her person, on articles belonging to her and in the caravan in which she had been staying.

The defence case was that it was clear that she had frequently lied to the police and no reliance could be placed upon the truth of any admissions she had made. Judith Ward was convicted on all counts.

After her trial, Judith Ward did not apply for leave to appeal against conviction or sentence, but in September 1991 the Home Secretary, being concerned about the validity of the scientific evidence at the trial, referred the matter to the Court of Appeal, pursuant to section 17(1)(a) of the *Criminal Appeal Act* 1968.

In *R v Ward* [1993] 1 W.L.R. 619, Judith Ward's appeal against conviction was allowed. It was held that by deliberately withholding experimental data on the ground that it might damage the prosecution case, three government scientists had failed in their clear duty to assist in a neutral and impartial way in a criminal investigation. It was also held that failing to disclose relevant records of interviews with Miss Ward, together with witness statements and medical reports which would have supported her defence, namely that the jury could not rely upon the truth of any admissions she had made, amounted to a material irregularity.

The Court of Appeal in *Ward* stated,

> *"Non-disclosure is a potent source of injustice and even with the benefit of hindsight, it will often be difficult to say whether or not an undisclosed item of evidence might have shifted the balance or opened a new line of defence."* (642)
>
> *"... We would adopt the words of Lawton L.J. in Reg. v. Hennessey (Timothy) (1978) 68 Cr.App.R. 419, 426, where he said that the courts must*
>
> *"keep in mind that those who prepare and conduct prosecutions owe a duty to the courts to ensure that all relevant evidence of help to an accused is either led by them or made available to the defence. [...]."*
>
> *That statement reflects the position in 1974 no less than today. We would emphasise that "all relevant evidence of help to the accused" is not limited to evidence which will obviously advance the accused's case. It is of help to the accused to have the opportunity of considering all the material evidence which the prosecution have gathered, and from which the prosecution have made their own selection of evidence to be led..."* (645)

The Court also made it clear that, in relation to public interest immunity, such decisions should not be made without reference to the court.

The Court of Appeal went on to state,

> *"What are the lessons to be learnt from this miscarriage of justice? The law is of necessity concerned with practical affairs, and it cannot effectively guard against all the failings of those who play a part in the criminal justice system. But that sombre realism does not relieve us, as judges, from persevering in the task to ensure that the law, practice and methods of trial should be developed so as to reduce the risk of conviction of the innocent to an absolute minimum...*
>
> *...we believe that the surest way of preventing the misuse of scientific evidence is by ensuring that there is a proper understanding of the*

> *nature and scope of the prosecution's duty of disclosure... The new rules are helpful. But it is a misconception to regard them as exhaustive: they do not in any way supplant or detract from the prosecution's general duty of disclosure in respect of scientific evidence. That duty exists irrespective of any request by the defence. It is also not limited to documentation on which the opinion or findings of an expert is based. It extends to anything which may arguably assist the defence. It is therefore wider in scope than the rule. Moreover, it is a positive duty, which in the context of scientific evidence obliges the prosecution to make full and proper inquiries from forensic scientists in order to ascertain whether there is discoverable material. Given the undoubted inequality as between prosecution and defence in access to forensic scientists, we regard it as of paramount importance that the common law duty of disclosure, as we have explained it, should be appreciated by those who prosecute and defend in criminal cases. And, if difficulties arise in a particular case, the court must be the final judge."* (675-676)

The Runciman Commission (1993)

The *Royal Commission on Criminal Justice ("the Runciman Commission") (1993) (Cm 2263)* also expressed concern about the widely publicised miscarriages of justice of the time,

> *"...In addition to the terrorist cases where the convictions were quashed in 1990 and 1991, there has been...a fourth case (Judith Ward) where the conviction was quashed in 1992. There has also been a number of cases not connected with terrorism, the most notable examples being those of the Broadwater Farm Three, Stefan Kiszko, and the Cardiff Three..."*

The Runciman Commission's recommendations led to the setting up of the Criminal Cases Review Commission, which we refer to in **Chapter Three**.

Significantly, Chapter 6 of the Runciman Commission's Report stated at page 95,

> *"49. … We strongly support the aim of the recent decisions to compel the prosecution to disclose everything that may be relevant to the defence's case. But we accept the evidence that we have received that the decisions have created burdens for the prosecution that go beyond what is reasonable. At present the prosecution can be required to disclose the existence of matters whose potential relevance is speculative in the extreme. Moreover, the sheer bulk of the material involved in many cases makes it wholly impracticable for every one of what may be hundreds of thousands of individual transactions to be disclosed.*
>
> *50. In our unanimous view a reasonable balance between the duties of the prosecution and the rights of the defence requires that a new regime be created with two stages of disclosure. The first stage, of primary disclosure, would subject to appropriate exceptions be automatic. The second stage, of secondary or further disclosure, would be made if the defence could establish its relevance to the case. Where the prosecution and defence disagreed on this aspect, the court would rule on the matter after weighing the potential importance of material to the defence."*

Following the recommendations of the Royal Commission, a statutory regime governing disclosure was introduced: the *Criminal Procedure and Investigations Act* 1996.

Criminal Procedure and Investigations Act 1996

The *Criminal Procedure and Investigations Act* 1996 ('CPIA') set out for the first time a statutory framework for the disclosure exercise in criminal cases.

Under section 3(1)(a) of the CPIA, the prosecution had to make "primary disclosure" of any material which had not previously been disclosed to the accused and which, in the prosecutor's opinion, might undermine the case for the prosecution against the accused. The prosecution also had to make "secondary disclosure" under section 7(2)(a) after receipt of a defence statement, of previously undisclosed material which might reasonably be expected to assist the accused's case.

Criminal Justice Act 2003

The *Criminal Justice Act* 2003 amended the CPIA, by making the disclosure test objective rather than subjective and replaced the "primary disclosure" and "secondary disclosure" stages with the wider concepts of "initial disclosure" and "continuing disclosure". We discuss these further in **Chapter Three.**

R v H

In *R v H* UKHL 3; [2004] 2 AC 134; [2004] 2 Cr.App.R. 10, the House of Lords gave guidance in relation to prosecution applications to withhold sensitive material from the defence. *R v H* made it clear that the trial judge on a Public Interest Immunity application was required to give detailed consideration to the material sought to be withheld, that an application made without notice to the defence was only to be made in exceptional circumstances and that exceptionally a special counsel may need to be appointed. We consider this case in more detail in **Chapter Ten.**

CPIA Code of Practice

The CPIA also made provision for the publication of a Code of Practice setting out how police officers were to record, retain and reveal to the prosecutor material obtained in a criminal investigation. The CPIA Code of Practice was published in 2005, followed by a revised version of the Code in 2015. The current version of CPIA Code of Practice was published in September 2020 and came into force on 31 December 2020.

Criminal Procedure Rules

The first version of the Criminal Procedure Rules came into force on 4 April 2005. Since the 2005 edition of the Rules, there have been a number of updates. Part 15 of the Criminal Procedure Rules 2020 applies in the magistrates' court and in the Crown Court. It sets out procedural requirements in relation to disclosure. By way of example, CrimPR 15.2 states,

> *"15.2.—(1) This rule applies where, under section 3 of the Criminal Procedure and Investigations Act 1996, the prosecutor—*
>
> > *(a) discloses prosecution material to the defendant; or*
> >
> > *(b) serves on the defendant a written statement that there is no such material to disclose.*
>
> *(2) The prosecutor must at the same time so inform the court officer."*

Lord Justice Gross's 'Review of Disclosure in Criminal Proceedings' (September 2011)

This review considered the practical operation of the CPIA disclosure regime, with a particular focus on the proportionality of the time and costs involved in cases generating a substantial amount of documentation. Ultimately, no change to the CPIA was recommended.

The Review stated that it did not favour, *"the adoption of a "keys to the warehouse" approach"* to disclosure, rather it pointed out that care should be taken in seizing more material than was necessary and that excessive detail in scheduling should be avoided.

Lord Justice Gross and Lord Justice Treacy's 'Further Review of Disclosure in Criminal Proceedings: sanctions for disclosure failure' (November 2012)

This review considered whether the sanctions for disclosure failures were adequate, but ultimately did not recommend the creation of any additional penalties against either the prosecution or the defence.

'Protocol and Good Practice Model: Disclosure of information in cases of alleged child abuse and linked criminal and care directions hearings' (October 2013)

This protocol, which came into force on 1st January 2014, was signed by the Senior Presiding Judge, the President of the Family Division and the DPP, and was also issued with the support of ACPO, HM Courts & Tribunals Service and the Association of Independent Local Safeguarding Children Board Chairs. The stated aims and objectives of the Protocol included the facilitation of, *"timely and consistent disclosure of information and documents from the Family Justice System to the police and/or the CPS."* (paragraph 3.5)

Attorney General's Guidelines on Disclosure (2013)

These Guidelines replaced the Attorney General's Guidelines on Disclosure issued in 2005, consolidating and abbreviating previous guidance that had been given.

'Judicial Protocol on the Disclosure of Unused Material in Criminal Cases' (2013)

The Judicial Protocol accompanied the Attorney General's Guidelines (2013) and the two documents were intended to be read together.

Magistrates' Court Disclosure Review (Judiciary of England and Wales, May 2014)

This Review was established to, *"consider the practical operation of the CPIA disclosure regime in criminal cases in the magistrates' courts, with a particular focus on the proportionality of the time and costs involved in that process."* (paragraph 5)

'Making it Fair – a Joint Inspection of the Disclosure of Unused Material in Volume Crown Court Cases' (18 July 2017)

This joint report between HM Crown Prosecution Service Inspectorate and HM Inspectorate of Constabulary made a number of findings including the following at paragraph 1.3,

> *"The inspection found that police scheduling (the process of recording details of both sensitive and non-sensitive material) is routinely poor, while revelation by the police to the prosecutor of material that may undermine the prosecution case or assist the defence case is rare. Prosecutors fail to challenge poor quality schedules and in turn provide little or no input to the police. Neither party is managing sensitive material effectively and prosecutors are failing to manage ongoing disclosure. To compound matters, the auditing process surrounding disclosure decision-making falls far below any acceptable standard of performance. The failure to grip disclosure issues early often leads to chaotic scenes later outside the courtroom, where last minute and often unauthorised disclosure between counsel, unnecessary adjournments and – ultimately – discontinued cases, are common occurrences. This is likely to reflect badly on the criminal justice system in the eyes of victims and witnesses."*

Mouncher Investigation Report (2017)

The Mouncher Investigation Report, written by Richard Horwell KC, was published in July 2017, and is required reading for anyone involved in the disclosure exercise in a large or complex case.

The report considered the disclosure errors that led to the collapse of a case against eight former South Wales police officers who investigated the murder of Lynette White. They were charged with perverting the course of justice for their role in the arrest and prosecution of five men, who later became known as the "Cardiff Five". Three of those five men were convicted in the trial that followed. They, in turn, became known as the "Cardiff Three" and were jailed for life in 1990. They were, however, freed in 1992 after their convictions for the killing were quashed. The actual murderer was identified years later through DNA evidence and eventually he pleaded guilty in 2003 to carrying out the murder, alone.

The 2011 trial (*R v 'Mouncher and others'*) of the police officers who were charged with perverting the course of justice relating to the 1990 convictions, collapsed after the prosecution offered no evidence. Prosecution counsel stated at the time that, *"The prosecution can no longer sustain a position maintaining that the court and the Defendants can have the required confidence in the disclosure process."* The Mouncher Investigation Report considered why prosecution counsel gave that indication and why the prosecution was abandoned as a result.

In the Report's conclusions, the following causes of the disclosure failures in that case were set out at paragraph 24.7:

> *"...poor management by the CPS at the beginning; instruction of counsel too junior in call and of too little experience; the inability of the criminal trial system to flush out disclosure issues and to bring them before the judge; too narrow a disclosure test applied; the late appointment of a trial judge resulting in a lack of early active management of the case; inadequate skills, training and experience of disclosure police officers (in particular Lead Disclosure Officers); inability to retain disclosure officers; lack of instruction to police officers as to how to deal with sensitive documents; over-reliance on disclosure counsel including in relation to matters outside their instructions; insufficient formality in making and recording advice; inadequate supervision of officers and of counsel; and a lack of appreciation of the*

significance for disclosure purposes of material generated within the investigation as opposed to material physically received from outside."

R v Liam Allan

Liam Allan was charged with multiple counts of rape and sexual assault after allegations were made against him in 2015 when he was a criminology student. The case was eventually dropped, in December 2017, three days into the trial, after it was discovered that there had been text messages from the complainant indicating that the sex had been consensual; including one message, which read, *"It wasn't against my will or anything."*

2018 assessment of pre-trial rape and serious sexual assault cases

In January 2018, following the collapse of the Liam Allan case, the Crown Prosecution Service announced that it was assessing all cases in England and Wales where someone had been charged with rape or a serious sexual assault. The review process included an assessment of 3,637 cases. Between 1 January and 13 February 2018, it was established that, in this period alone, 47 cases that had had issues in relation to disclosure had been stopped.

Attorney General's 'Review of the efficiency and effectiveness of disclosure in the criminal justice system' (November 2018)

This was published in November 2018. Ultimately the review concluded that although the CPIA 1996 itself provided an appropriate disclosure regime, in practice the system was not working as effectively or efficiently as it should. The Review referred at page 12 to,

> *"...investigators and prosecutors interpreting the disclosure test too narrowly or placing too much focus on what the defence asserts to be its case, disregarding other matters unknown to the defence that would be part of the defence case if only they were made aware of them or other possible defences which the facts might support."*

National Disclosure Improvement Plans

The National Disclosure Improvement Plan (NDIP) was first published on 26 January 2018. The foreword described it as, "*a joint plan, owned by the police service, the Crown Prosecution Service and the College of Policing*". The NDIP sought to address practical issues that would result in improved disclosure and a change in mindset. Since first publication, there have been a number of updates, the most recent of which was published on 23 March 2021 and which claimed that, "*In the last 12 months we have seen a continued reduction in cases which are failing for disclosure reasons and we anticipate further reductions as the changes brought in by the AG's Guidelines take effect.*"

Attorney General's Guidelines on Disclosure (2020)

The Attorney General's Guidelines on Disclosure 2020 came into force on 31 December 2020, and replaced those issued in 2013. The 2020 Guidelines introduced the theme of addressing disclosure in a, "*thinking manner*", formalising a duty on the defence to have to engage actively with the prosecution in the disclosure process. It also introduced categories of material where there was a rebuttable presumption of disclosure.

Annex A of the 2020 Guidelines provided expanded and updated guidance in relation to Digital Material.

Annex B provided a section on pre-charge engagement, which was defined as the "*voluntary engagement between the parties to an investigation after the first PACE interview, and before any suspect has been formally charged.*" The current version of this annex is key reading for any practitioner who acts in Pre-Charge matters.

Annex C contained a Disclosure Management Document (DMD) template, which included a suggested way of presenting how electronic material had been dealt with. The current version of this annex is key reading for any practitioner who is dealing with a case involving digital or historic material.

Attorney General's Guidelines on Disclosure (2022)

The Attorney General's Guidelines on Disclosure 2022 were published on 26 May 2022 and became effective on 25 July 2022. These Guidelines implemented the changes recommended by the Annual Disclosure Review 2021/2022 and replaced the AG's supplementary guidelines on Digital Material (2013).

Essentially, much of the content of the 2022 Guidelines remains unchanged from the 2020 version. In accordance with the Attorney-General's written statement dated 26 May 2022, the key changes to the Guidelines focused on four areas:

> *"1) **Third Party Material Access** – The provisions for accessing third party material are now expressed in a staged manner to aid with their application by busy investigators, disclosure officers and prosecutors. The principles are also strengthened in-line with the dicta of the Court of Appeal in R v Bater-James & Anor [2020] EWCA Crim 790. Investigators and prosecutors are also now explicitly required to keep written records of the reasons for making third party material requests, and to balance such requests with the privacy rights of those affected.*
>
> *2) **Material Presumed to Meet the Test for Disclosure** – This section of the guidelines has been subject to limited restructuring in order to clarify that material contained in a crime report need only be provided once, via the provision of the crime report, and need not be duplicated where it appears elsewhere. Important clarifications to the practicality of providing large video files, especially body worn videos, have also been made to aid investigators.*
>
> *3) **Defence Engagement** – Throughout the Guidelines, guidance as to how and when the defence should provide information to the prosecution has been clarified and where appropriate made more definitive.*

4) ***Redaction Annex*** *– A new annex has been added clarifying how investigators should meet their data protection obligations when providing material to the CPS for the purposes of a charging decision."*

Collapse of the Serco and Unaoil cases (2021)

On 26 April 2021, a fraud trial of two former executives of Serco collapsed following the Serious Fraud Office's failure to disclose key documents to the defence. The prosecution had sought an adjournment to try to remedy the disclosure failings but when this application was refused by the trial judge, the prosecution had no alternative but to offer no evidence. This had been a substantial case involving an allegation that the defendants had fraudulently hidden £12 million in profits on a contract for the electronic monitoring of offenders on behalf of the Ministry of Justice.

On 10 December 2021, just a few months after the collapse of the Serco case, the Court of Appeal allowed an appeal in another SFO prosecution, *R v Akle and another* [2021] EWCA Crim 1879, a case involving allegations of a conspiracy to give corrupt payments to public officials. The appeal was allowed on two grounds:

(i) That the Serious Fraud Office had failed to comply with its disclosure obligations (and that the trial judge had wrongly refused to order further disclosure) in relation to the SFO's contact with a 'fixer' who had entered into a plea arrangement with the US authorities. This was material that was capable of supporting the abuse of process application.

(ii) That the SFO's failure to comply with its disclosure obligations resulted in the appellant being unable to adduce evidence to show that a co-accused who had pleaded guilty, and whose pleas had been admitted into evidence, may not in fact have been guilty because he may have pleaded guilty due to improper pressure.

The Court of Appeal declined to order a retrial. Subsequently, Sir David Calvert-Smith provided a 106-page 'Independent Review into the Serious Fraud Office's handling of the Unaoil Case – R v Akle & Anor', which was published in July 2022. In paragraph 6, Chapter 11 of that Review, Sir David Calvert-Smith made the following observations:

> *"... The disclosure process, which is necessarily one which often dwarfs the actual gathering of directly relevant evidence, must be kept under constant review. When, as in this case, material which clearly should have been disclosed is only considered for disclosure following the receipt of a section 8 CPIA application, the result should be a much more generous interpretation of relevance than there had been before, instead of the gradual and apparently reluctant 'drip-feed' of disclosure which continued until the CACD hearing and resulted in the appeals of Akle and Bond being allowed... "*

Reflection upon the development of disclosure to-date demonstrates that problems arise from the practical difficulties in applying what is a relatively straightforward principle. The basic principle of disclosure is that in order for there to be a fair and legitimate verdict in any given case, the prosecution must provide the defence with material in its possession which might reasonably be considered capable of undermining the prosecution case or of assisting the defence case.

The purpose of disclosure is easy to state and is uncontroversial. However, the prosecution rarely now just have to consider whether, say, a single witness statement should be disclosed. Instead, the prosecution often must consider for disclosure the content of digital material; computer hard drives, mobile phones and sim cards, text, SMS and WhatsApp messages, email servers, social media accounts, internet history searches, CCTV, police Body Worn Video footage and financial data. It is not uncommon now for the quantity of the unused material to dwarf the served evidence.

That the current version of the Crown Prosecution Service's Disclosure Manual (Refreshed: 14 July 2022) runs to 38 Chapters and five annexes is indicative of the practical complexity involved in disclosure work.

Disclosure problems arise in the practical application of the law of disclosure and it is the practical application of the current disclosure regime to which we now turn to consider.

CHAPTER TWO

TERMINOLOGY

In this chapter we examine some of the language that is used when talking about disclosure.

One reason that the disclosure exercise is often misunderstood is that there is insufficient understanding of the terminology used in association with it. It is important, therefore, to use a common vocabulary when communicating about disclosure.

The Disclosure Test

The disclosure test is set out in section 3(1)(a) of the *Criminal Procedure and Investigations Act* 1996 and refers to the prosecutor's duty to disclose to the accused,

> *"any prosecution material which has not previously been disclosed to the accused and which might reasonably be considered capable of undermining the case for the prosecution against the accused or of assisting the case for the accused"*

The words of the disclosure test are simple and should not be given a gloss, for example by referring to a "strict" or "narrow" interpretation of the test.

It is also worth bearing in mind the reference to the words, "the case" for the prosecution and "the case" for the accused. So, for example, an analyst's chart that may have been generated in the course of the police investigation might be a helpful document in summarising certain aspects of the evidence but it would not strictly be disclosable if it did not undermine the prosecution case or assist the defence case.

"Disclosure" is defined in Chapter 1 of the CPS Disclosure Manual (Refreshed: 14 July 2022) as referring to,

> *"...providing the defence with copies of, or access to, any material which might reasonably be considered capable of undermining the case for the prosecution against the accused, or of assisting the case for the accused, and which has not previously been disclosed. The application of this test to relevant material is referred to in this manual as 'the Disclosure Test'. The duty on a prosecutor to review material is an ongoing one and the disclosure should be kept under continuous review throughout the proceedings.* ***Prosecutors should note that this test does not include an assessment as to whether the material is or could be admissible in a trial, or the merits of a defence."*** (emphasis added)

The last sentence makes it clear that, just because a document is unlikely to be admissible in evidence or that the defence raised is weak, these are not factors to take into consideration when determining whether the disclosure test is passed.

The importance of not simply looking at material from a prosecution perspective when considering the disclosure test, was highlighted by the Court of Appeal in *R v Gohil* [2018] 1 WLR 3697, where Gross LJ made the following observations at page 3726,

> *"132 When seeking to perform their duty in respect of disclosure, reference has already been made to counsel applying the "context" test ... Thus, documents were not disclosed, though disclosable when considered in isolation, if the overall context told against disclosure – because the full picture supported the Crown's case so that, in context, it was said, the material in question did not pass the test for disclosure...*
>
> *133 Some care is needed in this regard and, for our part, we think that the contrast between consideration of documents in isolation or in context, poses a false and distracting choice.*

134 In our judgment, the flaw ... was not that they sought to consider material in context. Material cannot sensibly be considered or evaluated other than in context. The flaw was instead a failure to see the material in question other than from the Crown's vantage point ... That counsel was confident that the Crown could rebut the inferences which might otherwise be drawn from the material undermining the Crown's case or assisting Gohil's case or casting doubt on the safety of his convictions, did not mean that the test for disclosure had not been passed."

Categories of material

In any criminal case, material can be divided into the following two categories:

- Evidence
- Unused Material

Unused material can, in turn, be broken down into three further sub-categories:

- Relevant Non-Sensitive Unused Material
- Relevant Sensitive Unused Material
- Non-Relevant Unused Material

Evidence

Evidence consists of the statements and exhibits relied on by the prosecution in support of its case and served on the defence. In the Crown Court, the evidence the prosecution relies on is uploaded to the Crown Court Digital Case System ('CCDCS' or DCS'). In the context of disclosure, the evidence is also sometimes referred to as the "used material", i.e. used in evidence. If it is not served in evidence, the material is, "unused".

Relevant material

The CPIA Code of Practice (2020) sets out the following relevancy test:

> *"material may be relevant to an investigation if it appears to an investigator, or to the officer in charge of an investigation, or to the disclosure officer, that it has some bearing on any offence under investigation or any person being investigated, or on the surrounding circumstances of the case, unless it is incapable of having any impact on the case"*

The CPIA Code of Practice (2020) defines "material" as follows:

> *"material is material of any kind, including information and objects, which is obtained or inspected in the course of a criminal investigation and which may be relevant to the investigation. This includes not only material coming into the possession of the investigator (such as documents seized in the course of searching premises) but also material generated by him (such as interview records)"*

It is worth bearing in mind the first sentence of this definition as it refers to "information", not just documentation. So, for example, if the prosecution have knowledge that a witness has just been charged with perjury in an unrelated case, that information is clearly disclosable.

Non-relevant material

As the name suggests, non-relevant material is all material falling outside the definition of relevant material above. It will very much depend on the issues in a particular case. By way of example, if paperwork seized during a police search of the defendant's address was found to include a file of children's homework, that homework file would likely be non-relevant material in, say, a fraud case. In a child abduction case, on the other hand, the existence of a child's homework at the address may be very relevant.

The prosecution, and in practice the disclosure officer, should keep the non-relevant material constantly under review as the defence are not provided with a list of the non-relevant material in a case. Care will need to be taken, particularly in larger and more complex cases, that the non-relevant material is reviewed in light of any new issues that arise as the case progresses.

Sensitive and Non-Sensitive Unused Material

The CPIA Code of Practice (2020) defines sensitive material as, *"material, the disclosure of which, the disclosure officer believes, would give rise to a real risk of serious prejudice to an important public interest"* and gives the following examples:

- *"material relating to national security;*
- *material received from the intelligence and security agencies;*
- *material relating to intelligence from foreign sources which reveals sensitive intelligence gathering methods;*
- *material given in confidence;*
- *material relating to the identity or activities of informants, or undercover police officers, or witnesses, or other persons supplying information to the police who may be in danger if their identities are revealed;*
- *material revealing the location of any premises or other place used for police surveillance, or the identity of any person allowing a police officer to use them for surveillance;*

- *material revealing, either directly or indirectly, techniques and methods relied upon by a police officer in the course of a criminal investigation, for example covert surveillance techniques, or other methods of detecting crime;*

- *material whose disclosure might facilitate the commission of other offences or hinder the prevention and detection of crime;*

- *material upon the strength of which search warrants were obtained;*

- *material containing details of persons taking part in identification parades;*

- *material supplied to an investigator during a criminal investigation which has been generated by an official of a body concerned with the regulation or supervision of bodies corporate or of persons engaged in financial activities, or which has been generated by a person retained by such a body;*

- *material supplied to an investigator during a criminal investigation which relates to a child or young person and which has been generated by a local authority social services department, an Area Child Protection Committee or other party contacted by an investigator during the investigation;*

- *material relating to the private life of a witness"*

If the unused material does not fall within the definition of sensitive material, but is relevant, it is referred to as "Relevant Non-Sensitive Unused Material".

Served

The term "served" is usually interpreted as meaning served as evidence on the defence. From a prosecution point of view, sometimes police officers may refer to material as having been "served" when what they really mean is that it has been provided to the CPS Reviewing Lawyer or **disclosed** to the defence. It is always worth clarifying in case there is any doubt when one party refers to material having been served, who it has been served on and whether what is meant is service of evidence or disclosure of unused material.

Another problem that can arise is when the police are under the mistaken impression that a statement or document has been served in evidence, when it has not been. If prosecuting, it may be helpful to provide the police (in particular the Officer in the Case and the designated Disclosure Officer) with a copy of the evidence indices, which can be downloaded from the Digital Case System, requesting cross referencing and identification of any omitted material.

Revelation to the prosecutor

The process of revelation of material to the prosecutor is set out in the CPIA Code of Practice (2020), paragraph 7.3 of which states that,

> *"The disclosure officer should draw the attention of the prosecutor to any material an investigator has retained…which it is considered may satisfy the test for prosecution disclosure in the Act, explaining the reasons for coming to that view."*

Investigator

Paragraph 2.1 of the CPIA Code of Practice (2020) provides the following definition:

> *"an investigator is any police officer involved in the conduct of a criminal investigation. All investigators have a responsibility for*

carrying out the duties imposed on them under this code, including in particular recording information, and retaining records of information and other material"

Officer in the Case ('OIC')

Paragraph 2.1 of the CPIA Code of Practice (2020) defines the officer in charge of an investigation, often referred to as the Officer in the Case or OIC, as follows,

> *"the officer in charge of an investigation is the police officer responsible for directing a criminal investigation. They are also responsible for ensuring that proper procedures are in place for recording information, and retaining records of information and other material, in the investigation".*

Disclosure Officer

Paragraph 2.1 of the CPIA Code of Practice (2020) provides the following definition:

> *"the disclosure officer is the person responsible for examining material retained by the police during the investigation; revealing material to the prosecutor during the investigation and any criminal proceedings resulting from it, and certifying that he has done this; and disclosing material to the accused at the request of the prosecutor"*

In less complex cases, the OIC will also designate themselves the task of Disclosure Officer. The larger and more complex a case, the greater the probability that the Disclosure Officer role will be assigned to a separate officer or officers, with a lead disclosure officer being responsible for oversight of the disclosure process including signing and dating the MG6Cs.

It is essential that the Disclosure Officer and the OIC are in close and regular contact to ensure that the disclosure process is being conducted effectively and that everyone is alive to the issues in the case as it develops.

Prosecutor

Paragraph 2.1 of the CPIA Code of Practice (2020) defines a 'prosecutor' as follows:

> *"the prosecutor is the authority responsible for the conduct, on behalf of the Crown, of criminal proceedings resulting from a specific criminal investigation"*

When defending in a Crown Court case, it is imperative that you identify at the outset, by reference to the Disclosure Management Document (DMD), which individuals have been designated to the aforementioned roles in the investigation.

MG6C or 'Police Schedule of Relevant Non-Sensitive Unused Material'

The police form setting out the schedule of relevant non-sensitive unused material is called the MG6C. A pro-forma has been included on the following page.

RESTRICTED (when complete

MG6C

POLICE SCHEDULE OF RELEVANT NON-SENSITIVE UNUSED MATERIAL

R v

URN				

The Disclosure Officer believes the following RELEVANT MATERIAL which does not form part of the prosecution case is NOT SENSITIVE. For further detailed guidance refer to the Disclosure Manual and Attorney General's Guidelines.

FOR CPS USE:
* Enter D = Disclose to defence
I = Item disclosable and defence may inspect
CND = Clearly not disclosable (by description)
ND = Document viewed and not disclosable

Item No.	Record below MATERIAL of any kind, including information and objects, which is obtained in the course of a criminal investigation and which may be relevant to the investigation; and RELEVANCE is that it has some bearing on any offence under investigation or any person being investigated or on the surrounding circumstances of the case, unless it is incapable of having any impact on the case. **Do not speculate. If it is not considered relevant do not record it on the schedule.** Give a sufficiently detailed DESCRIPTION of the relevant material for the prosecutor to make a decision on whether or not it should be examined.	LOCATION State precisely where the item can be found/located	*	REASON FOR DECISION
	The relevant material is:			
	The relevant material is:			
	The relevant material is:			
	The relevant material is:			
	The relevant material is:			
	The relevant material is:			
	The relevant material is:			
	The relevant material is:			
	The relevant material is:			
	The relevant material is:			

Signature: .... Name:

Date:

Reviewing lawyer signature: ....

Print Name:

Date

2010/11

RESTRICTED (when complete)

Page 1 of 1

The MG6C itself is not the unused material; it is the schedule setting out the unused material.

The following are some examples of unused material that might appear on an MG6C. These examples have been taken from Annex A of the Crown Prosecution Service Disclosure Manual (Refreshed: 21 October 2021):

Crime reporting and suspect identification

- 999 voice tape
- Exhibits not referred to in statements
- Post arrest photographs
- Details of other suspects arrested interviewed or questioned but not charged
- Audio/video tapes of interviews of witnesses
- Potential witnesses' details where no MG11 [statement] given
- CCTV, Body Worn Videos or other videos
- Media releases by police
- Fingerprint forms
- Witness album documentation
- ID procedure forms (except participant lists)
- Crime reports

- Incident log of messages
- Pocket books
- Custody records
- Letter of complaint of crime
- First description of all suspects however and wherever recorded.
- Material in police possession from third parties
- Plans or video of crime scene
- Details of whether any witness has sought or received a reward

<u>Administration</u>

- Road traffic crash reports
- Vulnerable victim or witness profile
- Record of property recovered from crime scenes
- Record of searches
- Post charge photograph
- Holmes actions, messages and documents
- Family liaison logs
- Property recovered from crime scenes forms

Investigation

- Scientific or SOCO findings not used as evidence
- Draft statements or preparatory notes
- DNA or other forensic material not used as evidence
- MG11s from unwilling or unhelpful witnesses
- Prompt notes for interviews
- Medical Examiner reports for suspect or witnesses
- Records of information provided e.g. in conversation
- House to house enquiries
- Audiotape or written note of interview with witnesses notified by the accused

Forensic and medical records

- SOCO/IDO work sheets
- File records
- Pathologist's records
- Dental records
- Forensic scientist's records / lab forms
- Hospital records relating to the condition which is the subject of the offence charged

Third party

- Medical and dental records
- Media material
- Special procedure applications
- Records held by other agencies
- Records/material held by Social Services or local authority

Schedule endorsements

The following endorsements are used to mark up the MG6C by the Reviewing Lawyer who must sign and date the schedule when completed:

1. **D** = **D**isclose to defence
2. **I** = Item disclosable and defence may **I**nspect
3. **CND** = **C**learly **N**ot **D**isclosable (by description)
4. **ND** = Document viewed and **N**ot **D**isclosable

The following extract from Chapter 12 of the CPS Disclosure Manual (Refreshed: 21 October 2021) provides further guidance in relation to marking up MG6Cs.

> *"Schedule endorsements*
>
> *When considering the initial duty to disclose, the prosecutor should record decisions on the MG6C, giving brief reasons for the decisions in the reasons column where:*

- *the question of whether the material meets the test for disclosure may not be apparent from the description;*
- *the prosecutor has decided to disclose material not identified by the disclosure officer on form MG6E as satisfying the disclosure test, or*
- *reasons might otherwise be helpful.*

The MG6C should be signed and dated by the prosecutor upon completion and the DRS noted accordingly.

Where an item satisfies the disclosure test and is to be disclosed, the prosecutor should in the appropriate column of the MG6C enter either:

- *a 'D', and indicate in the reasons section whether a copy is attached; or*
- *an 'I' where the item is to be disclosed and the prosecutor considers that inspection is more appropriate.*

Occasionally, items of unused material may be incorporated into the prosecution case. This should be identified on the schedule by endorsing the word 'evidence' alongside the item.

Where items are not disclosable the schedule may be endorsed with 'CND' – because the item is 'clearly not disclosable', or 'ND' – 'not disclosable'. The difference in endorsement depends upon whether or not the item has had to be viewed in order to take the decision on disclosure.

The expectation is that all items are described sufficiently to enable the prosecutor to make an informed decision on disclosure. Items that have an adequate description upon which to take a decision can be deemed 'clearly not disclosable' and should be marked 'CND'..."

It is important to note that a detailed description of an item on the MG6C is not a substitute for disclosing the document itself, if it passes the disclosure test. As Sir David Calvert-Smith noted at paragraph 61 of his 'Independent Review into the Serious Fraud Office's handling of the Unaoil Case – R v Akle & Anor' (2022),

> *"61. The purpose of the non-sensitive schedule (known as an MG6C) is to reveal to the defence the existence of material created and obtained during an investigation, together with the disclosure decision. Therefore, the inclusion of a description of that document on the schedule cannot of itself amount to disclosure. No good reason has been provided as to why, where so much time and effort was spent to include, in some cases though not all, a near-verbatim summary of the document, the underlying document was not disclosed."*

Defence practitioners should make it their practice to reflect carefully on the categorisation of the entries on the unused material schedule (MG6C) by the disclosure officer. Miscategorisation of items scheduled is a good indicator that the disclosure officer may have a poor understanding of the disclosure process.

MG6D or 'Police Schedule of Relevant Sensitive Material'

The police form setting out the schedule of relevant sensitive unused material is referred to as the MG6D. Unlike the MG6C, the MG6D is not supplied to the defence.

Examples of unused material that might be scheduled on an MG6D are also set out in Annex A of the CPS Disclosure Manual (Refreshed: 21 October 2021) and include:

- CHIS [Covert Human Intelligence Source] reports
- Offender profiles
- Port warnings

- Wanted/missing circulations
- Crimestoppers
- Force intelligence bureau material
- Sensitive material in police possession from Social Services or Local Authority
- Operational briefing/debriefing sheets
- Policy files
- Information in support of search or arrest warrants
- RIPA authorities / documentation
- Observations/surveillance logs

The following extract from Chapter 8 of the CPS Disclosure Manual (Refreshed: 21 October 2021) provides further guidance in relation to the content of MG6Ds:

> *"This schedule should be used to reveal to the prosecutor the existence of relevant unused material which the disclosure officer believes should be withheld from the defence. The disclosure officer must describe on the MG6D any relevant material which he or she believes would give rise to a real risk of serious prejudice to an important public interest if the existence of that material were revealed to the defence. The disclosure officer must also state the reason for that belief. This form will not be disclosed to the defence.*
>
> *In those cases where there is no sensitive unused material, the disclosure officer should endorse and sign an MG6D to this effect and should submit this together with the MG6C and MG6E."*

Disclosure Record Sheet ('DRS')

The CPS should, except in straightforward summary cases, complete a Disclosure Record Sheet (DRS). The DRS is designed to record chronologically all actions and decisions in relation to disclosure, including all pre-charge disclosure decisions. The DRS, which is an internal CPS document covering both sensitive and non-sensitive unused material, is not copied to the defence. Examples of what might be recorded on a DRS are as follows:

- any pre-charge discussions with the police concerning disclosure and reasonable lines of enquiry;
- receipt of the MG6 series;
- that a disclosure review has taken place and any actions taken in respect of inadequate schedules;
- the receipt and review of any addenda to the schedules;
- the completion and service of a Disclosure Management Document;
- contact with the disclosure officer or investigating officer in relation to sensitive unused material;
- receipt of a defence statement, the review of this and any actions sent for the investigator to undertake;
- any consultation with the prosecution advocate;
- any discussions with any other parties regarding unused material such as the court, the defence advocate or third parties;

- receipt of the prosecution advocate's advice in relation to unused material;
- details of any informal disclosure, should it occur; and
- the fact of any PII applications.

PII applications

A Public Interest Immunity (PII) application is an application to the court for a ruling that material or information that would otherwise pass the disclosure test need not be disclosed because it would cause a risk of serious prejudice to an important public interest. As an example, the prosecution may make a PII application in relation to the existence and identity of a police informant. PII applications are discussed in more detail in **Chapter Ten.**

MG6E

The MG6E is the police form containing the Disclosure Officer's Report and should include a signed certificate by him that he has retained all relevant material, has viewed the same and revealed it to the prosecutor in accordance with the CPIA.

The purpose of the MG6E is to flag up to the Reviewing Lawyer those items on the MG6C and MG6D which may satisfy the test for prosecution disclosure, explaining the reasons for coming to that view. Alternatively, the MG6E should certify that having reviewed all the relevant material, there is nothing that passes the disclosure test.

The police should give the prosecutor a copy of any material flagged up in the MG6E that has not previously been supplied. In particular, paragraph 7.4 of the CPIA Code of Practice (2020) specifically provides that the police should provide the prosecutor with any of the following:

- *"information provided by an accused person which indicates an explanation for the offence with which they have been charged;*
- *any material casting doubt on the reliability of a confession*
- *any material casting doubt on the reliability of a prosecution witness"*

The MG6E is an internal prosecution document and, like the MG6D, is not provided to the defence.

There should be an MG6E accompanying each and every MG6C and MG6D that is provided to the prosecutor. Any material listed on an MG6E should also be enclosed with it, so that that it can be read by the reviewing lawyer.

Certification by the disclosure officer

Chapter 10 of the CPS Disclosure Manual (Refreshed: 21 October 2021) refers to the requirement of the disclosure officer to provide certifications:

> *"The disclosure officer must provide different certifications in the course of the disclosure process, to cover:*
>
> - *revelation of all relevant retained material;*
> - *confirmation that no material falls within the categories to which the rebuttable presumption applies (if appropriate);*
> - *whether material satisfies the disclosure test; and*
> - *whether material satisfies the disclosure test following a defence statement as part of continuing duty.*
>
> *The case against each accused must be considered and certified separately.*

The purpose of certification is to provide an assurance to the prosecutor on behalf of the investigating team that all relevant material has been identified, considered and revealed to the prosecutor. Where the disclosure officer (or deputy disclosure officer) believes there is no material that satisfies the disclosure test, the officer should endorse the MG6E in the following terms: 'I have reviewed all the relevant material which has been retained and made available to me and there is nothing to the best of my knowledge and belief that might reasonably be considered capable of undermining the prosecution case against the accused or assisting the case for the accused.' Local arrangements apply for informing the prosecutor where no material falls within the categories to which the rebuttable presumption applies."

Disclosure Management Document

A Disclosure Management Document ('DMD') is mandatory in all Crown Court cases. The DMD is a key document for all parties, as it sets out the prosecution's approach to the unused material in a given case. It may, for example, set out:

- What reasonable lines of enquiry the prosecution have pursued and why.
- Details of the electronic material seized, how it has been examined and with what results.
- Steps taken by the prosecution to secure relevant material from third parties and with what results.

The defence should focus on the content of the DMD to consider whether it is adequate. If the DMD is inadequate the defence should bring this fact to the prosecution's attention. Further consideration of DMDs and a template are set out in **Chapter Eleven**.

Disclosure Strategy Document

This is similar to a Disclosure Management Document but is the internal police document used to set out their approach to the disclosure exercise, including any rationale for particular decisions taken. For prosecuting practitioners, review of the contents of this document is an effective way of establishing whether the designated disclosure officer has a sound grasp and understanding of the disclosure principals and whether they are likely to have been complied with in the case.

Initial Details of the Prosecution Case ('IDPC')

Initial Details of the Prosecution Case (IDPC) is required in all Magistrates' court cases, regardless of whether a defendant is to be eventually tried in the Magistrates' court or the Crown Court. The prosecutor must serve initial details of the prosecution case on the court officer as soon as possible and, in any event, no later than the beginning of the day of the first hearing. Where the defendant requests the IDPC, the prosecutor must also serve it on the defendant as soon as practicable and, in any event, no later than the beginning of the day of the first hearing. Where a defendant does not make such a request, the prosecutor still must make the IDPC available to the defendant at, or before, the beginning of the day of the first hearing. (CrimPR 8.2)

The IDPC is not the same as initial disclosure.

Please see **Chapter Six** for more details of the content of IDPCs and disclosure in the magistrates' court.

HOLMES

The Home Office Large Major Enquiry System (HOLMES) is a computer database designed to help investigations into large-scale criminal enquiries.

The revised Major Incident Room Standardised Administrative Procedures (MIRSAP) guidelines (2021) produced on behalf of ACPO (the Association of Chief Police Officers), provides a detailed description of the Holmes system. The 2021 MIRSAP Guidance is available online at:

https://library.college.police.uk/docs/NPCC/MIRSAP_V1_Nov_2021.pdf

Examples of the categories of documents included on a Holmes database include the following:

- Actions
- Statements
- Reports
- Interviews
- Personal Descriptive Forms
- Questionnaires
- House-to-House Documentation
- Messages
- Electronic Transmissions
- Intelligence Reports

Having looked at some of the most common terms used in discussing disclosure, we now turn to consider in more detail the key concepts of 'initial disclosure' and 'continuing disclosure'.

CHAPTER THREE

INITIAL, CONTINUING AND POST-TRIAL DISCLOSURE

This chapter sets out the key concepts of 'initial disclosure' and 'continuing disclosure'. We also consider the disclosure rules that apply post-trial.

The applicable disclosure regime

Although this book aims at setting out the current law on disclosure, it may be that you are involved in an old case where the CPIA does not apply. For ease of reference we set out the key dates:

- Where the investigation began before **1 April 1997**, the common law disclosure rules will apply.

- Where the investigation began on or after **1 April 1997** but before **4 April 2005**, the un-amended CPIA will apply, including the primary and secondary disclosure provisions.

- Where the investigation began on or after **4 April 2005**, then the CPIA, as amended by the CJA 2003, applies, i.e. the current disclosure provisions whereby primary and secondary disclosure have been replaced by initial and continuing disclosure.

- Section 6A(1)(ca) of the CPIA (which provides for the defence statement to set out particulars of the matters of fact on which a defendant intends to rely for the purposes of his defence) was inserted by section 60 of the *Criminal Justice and Immigration Act*

2008 and applies where the investigation began on or after 4 April 2005 and where a plea of not guilty has been entered (in the magistrates' court) or where the case has been committed, transferred (now allocated) or sent to the Crown Court on or after **3 November 2008**.

Moving from a subjective to an objective test

'Primary disclosure' and 'secondary disclosure' were the two stages referred to in the headings of sections 3 and 7 of the CPIA, before it was amended by the *Criminal Justice Act* 2003. The words, "primary disclosure" and "secondary disclosure" should no longer be used when referring to cases where the investigation began on or after 4 April 2005. They have been completely replaced by the wider concepts of 'initial disclosure' and 'continuing disclosure'.

The previous primary disclosure test was **subjective**, requiring the prosecutor to disclose any prosecution material which had not previously been disclosed which, *"in the **prosecutor's opinion** might undermine the case for the prosecution against the accused" (emphasis added).*

The initial disclosure duty is **objective** and includes a further duty to disclose material that helps the defence case. Section 3(1)(a) of the CPIA provides that the prosecutor must, "*disclose to the accused any prosecution material which has not previously been disclosed to the accused and which might reasonably be considered capable of undermining the case for the prosecution against the accused or of assisting the case for the accused*".

The prosecution's continuing duty to review disclosure, contained in section 7A of the CPIA, replaces the old 'secondary disclosure' provisions of section 7, which were previously only triggered following service of a defence statement. However, even though a defence statement is not now required to trigger the prosecution's continuing duty to review disclosure; service of a defence statement will, in practical terms, prompt the prosecution to review the unused material again in a more focused way.

Paragraph 8.3 of the CPIA Code of Practice (2020) provides that,

> *"8.3 In particular, after a defence statement has been given, or details of the issues in dispute have been recorded on the Preparation for Effective Trial form or the Plea and Trial Preparation Hearing form, the disclosure officer must look again at the material which has been retained and must draw the attention of the prosecutor to any material which might reasonably be considered capable of undermining the case for the prosecution against the accused or of assisting the case for the accused…"*

Initial duty to disclose

Section 3 of the CPIA states,

> ***"3 Initial duty of prosecutor to disclose.***
>
> *(1) The prosecutor must –*
>
> *(a) disclose to the accused any prosecution material which has not previously been disclosed to the accused and which might reasonably be considered capable of undermining the case for the prosecution against the accused or of assisting the case for the accused, or*
>
> *(b) give to the accused a written statement that there is no material of a description mentioned in paragraph (a).*
>
> *(2) For the purposes of this section prosecution material is material—*
>
> *(a) which is in the prosecutor's possession, and came into his possession in connection with the case for the prosecution against the accused, or*
>
> *(b) which, in pursuance of a code operative under Part II, he has inspected in connection with the case for the prosecution against the accused.*

(3) Where material consists of information which has been recorded in any form the prosecutor discloses it for the purposes of this section—

(a) by securing that a copy is made of it and that the copy is given to the accused, or

(b) if in the prosecutor's opinion that is not practicable or not desirable, by allowing the accused to inspect it at a reasonable time and a reasonable place or by taking steps to secure that he is allowed to do so;

and a copy may be in such form as the prosecutor thinks fit and need not be in the same form as that in which the information has already been recorded.

(4) Where material consists of information which has not been recorded the prosecutor discloses it for the purposes of this section by securing that it is recorded in such form as he thinks fit and—

(a) by securing that a copy is made of it and that the copy is given to the accused, or

(b) if in the prosecutor's opinion that is not practicable or not desirable, by allowing the accused to inspect it at a reasonable time and a reasonable place or by taking steps to secure that he is allowed to do so.

(5) Where material does not consist of information the prosecutor discloses it for the purposes of this section by allowing the accused to inspect it at a reasonable time and a reasonable place or by taking steps to secure that he is allowed to do so.

(6) Material must not be disclosed under this section to the extent that the court, on an application by the prosecutor, concludes it is not in the public interest to disclose it and orders accordingly.

> *(7) Material must not be disclosed under this section to the extent that it is material the disclosure of which is prohibited by section 56 of the Investigatory Powers Act 2016.*
>
> *(8) The prosecutor must act under this section during the period which, by virtue of section 12, is the relevant period for this section."*

Initial disclosure is provided by the CPS in correspondence, under the cover of a letter often referred to by practitioners as, *"the section 3 letter"*. An example of a section 3 letter is set out at the end of this chapter.

Timing of initial disclosure

There is as yet no prescribed time period, under section 12, for the prosecution to provide initial disclosure. Accordingly, and pursuant to section 13 of the CPIA, the prosecution must act under section 3, *"as soon as is reasonably practicable"*. In any event, the court will usually set a date by which initial disclosure is to be completed. In the magistrates' court, this is usually 28 days following entry of a not guilty plea. In the Crown Court, the prosecution are usually ordered at the PTPH to complete initial disclosure within 50 days of the case being sent in custody cases and 70 days after sending in bail cases. This is referred to as the Stage 1 date on the PTPH form, a copy of which is enclosed at the end of this chapter.

The Attorney General's Guidelines on Disclosure (2022) provide the following further guidance in relation to the timing of service of initial disclosure:

> ***"Cases expected to be tried in the magistrates' courts***
>
> *102. Where a case is charged on the Full Code Test and a not guilty plea is anticipated, initial disclosure should be served in advance of the first hearing.*

103. Where a guilty plea was originally anticipated but a not guilty plea is entered then initial disclosure should be served as soon as possible after a not guilty plea is entered.

104. Where a case is charged on the Threshold Test, initial disclosure should be served as soon as possible after the Full Code Test is applied and in accordance with any order made by the court.

Cases sent to the Crown Court for trial

105. Where it is expected that the accused will maintain a not guilty plea, it is encouraged as a matter of best practice for initial disclosure to be served prior to the Plea and Trial Preparation Hearing (PTPH).

106. It is accepted that it may not be appropriate or possible to serve initial disclosure prior to the PTPH for cases charged on the Threshold Test. Where initial disclosure has not been served at the PTPH it should be served as soon as possible after that hearing and in accordance with any direction made by the court.

107. In cases prosecuted by the Serious Fraud Office, or other similarly large or complex cases, it is accepted that full initial disclosure may not be capable of being served prior to the PTPH. In such cases, best practice is to adopt a phased approach to disclosure, ensuring that robust judicial case management during Further Case Management Hearings, and in line with the Criminal Procedure Rules and Criminal Practice Directions, manages the on-going disclosure process. Utilising an initial DMD at the PTPH which outlines the intended plan for onwards staged disclosure of remaining materials and associated schedules, can be an effective mechanism for this approach and is to be adopted where possible."

Continuing duty to disclose

Section 7A of the CPIA states,

> *"7A Continuing duty of prosecutor to disclose*
>
> *(1) This section applies at all times—*
>
> *(a) after the prosecutor has complied with section 3 or purported to comply with it, and*
>
> *(b) before the accused is acquitted or convicted or the prosecutor decides not to proceed with the case concerned.*
>
> *(2) The prosecutor must keep under review the question whether at any given time (and, in particular, following the giving of a defence statement) there is prosecution material which—*
>
> *(a) might reasonably be considered capable of undermining the case for the prosecution against the accused or of assisting the case for the accused, and*
>
> *(b) has not been disclosed to the accused.*
>
> *(3) If at any time there is any such material as is mentioned in subsection (2) the prosecutor must disclose it to the accused as soon as is reasonably practicable…*
>
> *(4) In applying subsection (2) by reference to any given time the state of affairs at that time (including the case for the prosecution as it stands at that time) must be taken into account.*
>
> *(5) Where the accused gives a defence statement under section 5, 6 or 6B—*
>
> *(a) if as a result of that statement the prosecutor is required by this section to make any disclosure, or further disclosure, he must do so*

during the period which, by virtue of section 12, is the relevant period for this section;

(b) if the prosecutor considers that he is not so required, he must during that period give to the accused a written statement to that effect.

(6) For the purposes of this section prosecution material is material—

(a) which is in the prosecutor's possession and came into his possession in connection with the case for the prosecution against the accused, or

(b) which, in pursuance of a code operative under Part 2, he has inspected in connection with the case for the prosecution against the accused.

(7) Subsections (3) to (5) of section 3 (method by which prosecutor discloses) apply for the purposes of this section as they apply for the purposes of that.

(8) Material must not be disclosed under this section to the extent that the court, on an application by the prosecutor, concludes it is not in the public interest to disclose it and orders accordingly.

(9) Material must not be disclosed under this section to the extent that it is material the disclosure of which is prohibited by section 56 of the Investigatory Powers Act 2016."

[Section 6B, referred to in subsection (5) above, is not yet in force. Section 56 of the *Investigatory Powers Act* 2016 relates to intercept material.]

There is also, as yet, no prescribed time period, under section 12, for the prosecution to respond to the defence statement. Accordingly, and pursuant to section 13 of the CPIA, the prosecution must provide disclosure in response to the defence statement, or confirm that there is no disclosure arising, *"as soon as is reasonably practicable"* after the accused provides a defence statement.

In any event, the court will usually set a date by which the prosecution are to respond to the defence statement. In the Crown Court this is invariably the Stage 3 date, which is set at the PTPH. This is usually 14 days after the date fixed for service of the defence statement in custody cases, or 28 days thereafter in bail cases. Please see PTPH form at the end of this chapter.

Paragraph 129 of The Attorney General's Guidelines on Disclosure (2022) underscores that, *"The obligation of continuing disclosure is crucial and particular attention must be paid to understanding the significance of developments in the case on the unused material and earlier disclosure decisions.... The obligation is a continuous one, and it can be beneficial for it to take place in tranches, particularly in large and/or complex cases."*

Paragraph 130 of the Guidelines goes on to state, *"In particular, prosecutors should consider any issues raised by the defence at the first hearing in the magistrates' court or the PTPH in the Crown Court, as well as during any further hearings and after receipt of a defence statement. Any matters raised on the preparation for effective trial form or the PTPH form should also be carefully considered."*

An example of a letter responding to the defence statement is set out at the end of this chapter.

Cut-throat defences

A good practical example of continuing disclosure is where it becomes apparent for the first time in a multi-handed case that one or more of the defendants is running a cut-throat defence. Such a defence should be set out in the defence statement. Sometimes, however, such a defence may arise during the trial itself.

As soon as the prosecution are aware of a cut-throat defence, this should trigger a review of the unused for material that may assist D1 who is cutting D2's throat and vice versa. The review may also lead to the disclosure of a co-defendant's defence statement. This is considered further in **Chapter Four** in the context of the Court of Appeal decision in *R v Cairns* [2002] EWCA Crim 2838.

Use of disclosed material

It is worth bearing in mind that material that is disclosed must not be misused. Section 17 of the CPIA states,

> *"17 Confidentiality of disclosed information.*
>
> *(1) If the accused is given or allowed to inspect a document or other object under—*
>
> *(a) section 3, 4, 7A, 14 or 15, or*
>
> *(b) an order under section 8,*
>
> *then, subject to subsections (2) to (4), he must not use or disclose it or any information recorded in it.*
>
> *(2) The accused may use or disclose the object or information—*
>
> *(a) in connection with the proceedings for whose purposes he was given the object or allowed to inspect it,*
>
> *(b) with a view to the taking of further criminal proceedings (for instance, by way of appeal) with regard to the matter giving rise to the proceedings mentioned in paragraph (a), or*
>
> *(c) in connection with the proceedings first mentioned in paragraph (b).*
>
> *(3) The accused may use or disclose—*

(a) the object to the extent that it has been displayed to the public in open court, or

(b) the information to the extent that it has been communicated to the public in open court;

but the preceding provisions of this subsection do not apply if the object is displayed or the information is communicated in proceedings to deal with a contempt of court under section 18.

(4) If—

(a) the accused applies to the court for an order granting permission to use or disclose the object or information, and

(b) the court makes such an order,

the accused may use or disclose the object or information for the purpose and to the extent specified by the court.

(5) An application under subsection (4) may be made and dealt with at any time, and in particular after the accused has been acquitted or convicted or the prosecutor has decided not to proceed with the case concerned; but this is subject to rules made by virtue of section 19(2).

(6) Where—

(a) an application is made under subsection (4), and

(b) the prosecutor or a person claiming to have an interest in the object or information applies to be heard by the court,

the court must not make an order granting permission unless the person applying under paragraph (b) has been given an opportunity to be heard.

(7) References in this section to the court are to—

(a) a magistrates' court, where this Part applies by virtue of section 1(1);

(b) the Crown Court, where this Part applies by virtue of section 1(2).

(8) Nothing in this section affects any other restriction or prohibition on the use or disclosure of an object or information, whether the restriction or prohibition arises under an enactment (whenever passed) or otherwise."

Section 18(1) of the CPIA states that,

"It is a contempt of court for a person knowingly to use or disclose an object or information recorded in it if the use or disclosure is in contravention of section 17."

If the prosecution express any concerns about disclosing certain material to the defence, the prosecutor can be reminded by the defence that they are in any event prevented from misusing such material and could be found in contempt of court if they did so. Care should be taken, therefore, that there is not an overreliance on data protection justifications for editing or not disclosing material.

Post-conviction disclosure

Although the prosecution's continuing disclosure duty under section 7A of the CPIA concludes at the end of the trial, there are still disclosure obligations on the prosecution under common law after a defendant is convicted, principally in two respects:

- Disclosure relevant to sentence
- Disclosure relevant to the safety of the conviction

Disclosure relevant to sentence

Paragraph 139 of the Attorney General's Guidelines on Disclosure (2022) provides that,

> *"At sentence, the prosecutor should disclose any material which might reasonably be considered capable of ensuring fairness in the sentencing process. This material could include information which might mitigate the seriousness of the offence or the level of the defendant's involvement."*

Disclosure relevant to the safety of the conviction

Paragraph 140 of the Attorney General's Guidelines on Disclosure (2022) provides that,

> *"Where, at any stage after the conclusion of the proceedings, material comes to light which might reasonably be considered capable of casting doubt upon the safety of the conviction, the prosecutor should disclose such material."*

The leading case on the disclosure duties placed on the prosecution post-conviction is the Supreme Court decision of *R (Nunn) v. Chief Constable of Suffolk Police (JUSTICE and others intervening)* [2015] AC 225. Lord Hughes JSC stated at paragraph 35,

> *"There can be no doubt that if the police or prosecution come into possession, after the appellate process is exhausted, of something new which might afford arguable grounds for contending that the conviction was unsafe, it is their duty to disclose it to the convicted defendant. Simple examples might include a new (and credible) confession by someone else, or the discovery, incidentally to a different investigation, of a pattern, or of evidence, which throws doubt on the original conviction. Sometimes such material may appear unexpectedly and adventitiously; in other cases it may be the result of a re-opening by the police of the inquiry. In either case, the new material is likely to*

> *be unknown to the convicted defendant unless disclosed to him. In all such cases, there is a clear obligation to disclose it."*

Criminal Cases Review Commission

The Supreme Court in *Nunn* made it clear that the disclosure obligations on the prosecution under common law post-conviction were not the same as the CPIA obligations that applied before and during the trial. The Supreme Court also pointed to the safety net of the Criminal Cases Review Commission,

> *"…the Criminal Cases Review Commission… has the power to review any conviction and which is charged, if it thinks that there is a real possibility that the Court of Appeal might quash the conviction, with the power to refer the case back to the court for, exceptionally, the hearing of a second appeal – and on any grounds, whether the same as before or different. Such a referral by-passes the requirement for leave to appeal. An arguable case is assumed. The court thereupon has the duty to investigate the safety of the conviction and must quash it if it is unsafe. The CCRC's extensive investigative powers include the power to require the production to it of any material in the hands of the police or any other public body, to appoint an investigator with all the powers of a police officer, and to assemble fresh evidence not before the court of trial."* (paragraph 20)

In *R v Gohil* [2018] 1 WLR 3697, a case in which the defendants applied to reopen the final determinations of the Court of Appeal on the grounds that the Court of Appeal had been misled by the Crown's failure to disclose relevant material, Gross LJ stated at page 3725,

> *"As it seems to us, complaints as to non-disclosure and the emergence of fresh evidence following concluded proceedings, may properly be viewed as paradigm cases for the CCRC, the more especially where investigation is required or would be beneficial."*

Having considered the prosecution's duty to carry out initial, continuing and, in some circumstances, even post-trial disclosure, we turn in the next chapter to consider obligations that are placed on the defence to provide a defence statement and witness notice.

Pro-forma initial disclosure (section 3) letter

LETTER TO DEFENCE WHERE THERE IS [NO] MATERIAL TO DISCLOSE (CROWN COURT)

I am required to disclose to you any prosecution material which has not previously been disclosed, and which might reasonably be considered capable of undermining the prosecution case against the accused or of assisting the case for the accused.

Attached to this letter is a copy of a schedule of non-sensitive unused material. The disclosure officer in this case is …

Where the word 'evidence' appears alongside any item, the items listed on the schedule are intended to be used as part of the prosecution case. You will receive a written notice should the position change.

[At this stage, there is no prosecution material which requires disclosure to you.]

or

[Where indicated, copies of the items listed are attached. Material marked as available for inspection can be viewed by arrangement with the disclosure officer.

This material is disclosed to you in accordance with the provisions of the Criminal Procedure and Investigations Act 1996 (CPIA), and you must not use or disclose it, or any information recorded in it, for any purpose other than in connection with these criminal proceedings. If you do so without the permission of the court, you may commit an offence.

It is essential that you preserve this schedule in its present form, as access to any material will only be granted upon its production to the disclosure officer.]

If you supply a written defence statement to me and to the court within 28 days, any undisclosed material will be further reviewed in the light of that statement.

The defence statement must comply with the requirements of section 6A of the CPIA:

> (1) For the purposes of this Part a defence statement is a written statement—
>
> > (a) setting out the nature of the accused's defence, including any particular defences on which he intends to rely,
> >
> > (b) indicating the matters of fact on which he takes issue with the prosecution,
> >
> > (c) setting out, in the case of each such matter, why he takes issue with the prosecution,
> >
> > [(ca) setting out particulars of the matters of fact on which he intends to rely for the purposes of his defence, and]
> >
> > (d) indicating any point of law (including any point as to the admissibility of evidence or an abuse of process) which he wishes to take, and any authority on which he intends to rely for that purpose.
>
> (2) A defence statement that discloses an alibi must give particulars of it, including—
>
> > (a) the name, address and date of birth of any witness the accused believes is able to give evidence in support of the alibi, or as many

of those details as are known to the accused when the statement is given;

(b) any information in the accused's possession which might be of material assistance in identifying or finding any such witness in whose case any of the details mentioned in paragraph (a) are not known to the accused when the statement is given.

A defence statement is required in Crown court cases. In accordance with my continuing duty, I will review the information you provide in the statement to identify any remaining material which has not already been disclosed. The statement will also be relied on by the court if you later make an application under section 8 CPIA.

If you do not make a CPIA-compliant defence statement where one is required or provided, or do so late, the court may hear comment and/or draw an adverse inference.

You are also required to give advance details of any witnesses you intend to call at trial within 28 days, which can be extended on application. If you do not give details, or do so late, the court may comment and/or draw an adverse inference.

Example of a letter in response to a defence statement

Disclosure of Prosecution Material under Section 7A Criminal Procedure and Investigations Act 1996

I have considered your defence statement [dated...] provided under Section 5/section 6 Criminal Procedure and Investigations Act 1996 (CPIA). Under section 7A CPIA I am required to disclose to you any prosecution material which has not been previously been disclosed and which might reasonably be expected to assist your defence, as described in your statement.

A copy of a schedule of non-sensitive unused material prepared by the police has already been sent to you. The items listed below are those which I consider might reasonably be expected to assist your defence, as described in your statement, and which have not already been disclosed to you. The numbers refer to the numbers on the schedule previously provided. Where indicated, copies of the items listed are attached.

Item	Description	Copy
...	...	Attached
...	...	Attached

This material is disclosed to you in accordance with the provisions of the CPIA, and you must not use or disclose it, or any information recorded in it for any purpose other than in connection with these criminal proceedings. If you do so without the permission of the court, you may commit an offence.

If you consider that there is other prosecution material which might assist your defence and which has not already been disclosed, please let me know and I will reconsider my decision in the light of any further information that you provide. Alternatively, you may apply to the court under section 8 CPIA. The court will assess your application in the light of your defence statement.

If you request access to any item which has been marked for disclosure by inspection, it is essential that you preserve this letter in its present form, as access will only be granted upon production of this letter and the schedule previously provided to the person supervising access.

FORM - PTPH NG 2

PLEA AND TRIAL PREPARATION HEARING
PARTIES PRE-HEARING INFORMATION FORM

The pre-hearing information form must be completed by the parties for all cases sent to the Crown Court where a trial is anticipated unless the case is expressly exempted by the CrimPR or CrimPD.

Crown Court at:		T:	PTI URN:

	Defendant	*DOB*	*Principal Charge(s)*	☑ *Remand Status*	*Custody Time Limit*	*Date of Sending*
D1				☐ Unconditional bail ☐ Conditional Bail ☐ Custody ☐ Youth Det. Remand		

Contact Information

Court Case Progression	*Name*	*Phone*	*Email*
Case Progression Officer			

Prosecution Contacts	*Name*	*Phone*	*Email*
Advocate at PTPH			
Advocate for trial			
Reviewing Lawyer			
Case Progression Officer (usually Paralegal)			
Officer in the Case			

Defence Contacts		*Name and Address for Service*	*Phone*	*Secure email for service*
D1	Defence Solicitors (or unrepresented defendant)			
	Case Progression Officer			
	Advocate at PTPH			
	Advocate for trial			
	Funding – Tick ☑	Private Funding ☐; Legal Rep applied for ☐; Legal Rep Order granted ☐; or Unrepresented ☐		

V2.9 (03/07/2019)

FORM - PTPH NG 2

Prosecution Information for PTPH

	Yes/No/N/A	*If not yet served they can be served by/Notes*
Draft Indictment		
Summary of circumstances of the offence(s) and of any account given by defendant(s) in interview (this may be in Form MG5)		
Statements identified by prosecution as being of importance for the purpose of plea and initial case management		
Exhibits identified by prosecution as being of importance for the purpose of plea and initial case management		
Relevant CCTV that would be relied upon by prosecution at trial		
Streamlined Forensic Report(s) or indication of scientific evidence that the prosecution is likely to introduce		
Indication of medical evidence that the prosecution is likely to introduce		
Indication of other expert evidence that the prosecution is likely to introduce		
Indication of bad character evidence to be relied on		
Indication of any hearsay evidence to be relied on		
Indication of special measures to be sought		
Defendant's criminal record if any		
Victim Personal Statement if any		
Has a Disclosure Management Document been provided?		
Does the Prosecution believe that any third party holds potentially disclosable material?		
Will the prosecution be making enquiries to review that material?		

Defence Information for PTPH

D1		
Defence time estimate for trial (to include jury retirement)		
Real Issues Defence to summarise so far as known, the real issues in the case CrimPR 3.2;3.3;3.11		
	Yes/No/N/A	*Particulars*
Was the defendant under 18 at sending?		
Is the defendant vulnerable for a reason other than or additional to youth?		
Is the defendant said to be a victim of modern slavery?		
Streamlined Forensic Reports Defence to confirm whether the conclusions of any served Streamlined Forensics Report (SFR1) are admitted as fact. If not identify the disputed issues concerning that conclusion? Make clear		

V2.9 (03/07/2019)

FORM - PTPH NG 2

what is admitted and what is not admitted		
Disclosure Management Document if served	If responses may raise concerns about cross-disclosure they may be uploaded separately to the DCS: Defence Statement section for review at PTPH.	
Is any served DMD adequate and if not why not?		
Do the defence agree the reasonable lines of enquiry and, if not, what other lines of enquiry are suggested by the defence?		
Do the defence agree the level of extraction of data and, if not, what level is said to be necessary by reference to the issues in the case?		
Third Party Are there areas of third party disclosure that need to be pursued?		
Preliminary Issues Are there preliminary issues such as abuse of process or fitness to participate in trial process?		
Dismissal Is an application for dismissal anticipated after time for service elapses?		
Severance Is an application for severance anticipated? CrimPR 3.21		
Arraignment Can the defendant be arraigned at PTPH?		
Alternative Plea Is the defendant willing to offer a plea to another offence and/or a plea on a limited basis?		

All Parties: Information about Other Proceedings

Particulars of any associated CRIMINAL proceedings?	
Particulars of any linked FAMILY proceedings?	

V2.9 (03/07/2019)

FORM - PTPH NG 2

PLEA AND TRIAL PREPARATION HEARING JUDICIAL ORDERS

This form is the primary record of all orders made at PTPH and its completion is a judicial function.
All orders of the court at PTPH must be incorporated but any subsequent variation must be by further order.

Crown Court at:		T:	PTI URN:

Judge			
HHJ/Recorder:		Date:	

Witness and Intermediary Requirements Known at PTPH:

How to complete:

Availability and Listing: Witness and intermediary availability dates should be available at the PTPH. Parties should request a fixture if there is a witness under 10, OR there is a witness or defendant under 18 or vulnerable for some other reason, OR where a future intermediary application is anticipated.

Prosecution Witnesses required to attend: To be populated with names of prosecution witnesses whose statements have been uploaded to the DCS at PTPH.

Prosecution to indicate any witness whom the Prosecution intend to call live regardless of Defence requirements (write "**P**" in the "Required by" column).

Each Defendant is required to identify which prosecution witnesses it can be predicted will be required to give evidence by that defendant (write "**D1**" etc as appropriate in the relevant column) AND where a witness is required identify the relevant disputed issue for **that** defendant.

Parties are expected to provide a considered list and must not simply indicate "all witnesses". Where a witness is named but no statement has been provided parties are not expected to indicate requirements.

Witness Orders: Witness warning will be as confirmed by the Judge at PTPH. The Court has agreed that prosecution witnesses marked as confirmed are likely to be required to give evidence.

Unless otherwise ordered the Defence must also serve a Standard Witness Table at Stage 2.

Where it can be done justly at PTPH without further formality the judge may make orders such as:
- SMEAS – Special measures in which case the Court should specify which special measures are provided for;
- SUMM – ordering the issue of a witness summons for the witness where grounds are made out;
- UKLINK – ordering a UK live link if available – for example for police officers, other investigators, or experts to give evidence remotely;
- SAT – ordering a satellite link from abroad.

Intermediaries: If intermediaries have been identified at PTPH then the details should be inserted here, their availability information should be available, and the judge can make such orders as can be made at PTPH.

Young/Vulnerable Defendants: The judge may use this section to make and record measures required to assist the defendant to participate in the trial process the need for which is identified at PTPH.

V2.9 (03/07/2019)

FORM - PTPH NG 2

Prosecution Witnesses Required to Attend				
Name of prosecution witness	*Required to attend by*	*Relevant disputed issue etc.*	Confirmed by Court	SMEAS & Additional Judicial Orders
			☐	
			☐	
			☐	
			☐	
			☐	
			☐	
			☐	
			☐	
			☐	
			☐	
			☐	
			☐	
			☐	
			☐	

Intermediary Known at PTPH				
Prosecution or Defendant	*Name of Intermediary known at PTPH*	*Witness for whom intermediary appointed*	Confirmed by Court	SMEAS & Additional Judicial Orders
			☐	
			☐	
			☐	

Young/Vulnerable/Intimidated Defendants - Measures to assist that can be granted at PTPH	
The Court is required to give reasons for departing from the relevant provisions of the CrimPD – See CrimPD I 3D-3G and 3N; CrimPD V 18A-B – R v Grant-Morris [2017] EWCA Crim 1228 and the Equal Treatment Bench Book	
These directions apply to the following defendant(s)	**Name(s)**
During court proceedings the defendant is to be referred to as	**Name**
Measures that can be granted at PTPH without formal application: CrimPD 3C-3G These measures apply to pre-trial hearings as appropriate ☑	**Publicity about the Defendant** ☐ An order is made under s.45 YJCEA restricting publicity of name, address, school or other educational establishment, place of work or any still or moving picture or other matter likely to lead members of the public to identify the defendant whilst under the age of 18 OR ☐ An order has already been made under s.45 YJCEA restricting publicity of name, address, school or other educational establishment, place of work or any still or moving picture or other matter likely to lead members of the public to identify the defendant whilst under the age of 18 OR ☐ Separate order(s) have been made elsewhere under other provisions restraining publicity likely to identify the defendant (e.g. Contempt of Court Act) OR ☐ No order has been made in this case restraining publicity about the defendant **Severance** - Where the defendant appears alongside a defendant who is not vulnerable ☐ The court finds that the defendant should be tried alone OR

V2.9 (03/07/2019)

	☐ The court is satisfied that, with appropriate measures, the vulnerable defendant can be tried alongside the other(s) OR ☐ Does not apply in this case **Ground Rules Hearing** ☐ A Ground Rules Hearing will be required directions for which are made below OR ☐ No Ground Rules Hearing will be required **Intermediary** ☐ In this case a formal application will be required at Stage 2 if an intermediary is sought for the defendant OR ☐ Intermediary for pre-trial preparation granted ☐ Intermediary for pre-trial court visit granted ☐ Intermediary for whole of trial granted ☐ Intermediary for period when defendant may give evidence granted OR ☐ No intermediary required **Non-Trial Hearings – Suitability of Video Link** ☐ When attendance required defendant to be produced in person OR ☐ When attendance required defendant may be produced by video-link **Other** ☐ Arrangements to be made between Defence and Court Staff, and if necessary the Police, so that defendant not exposed to intimidation, vilification or abuse when attending court ☐ Suitable supporting adult (such as parent, support worker or other appropriate person approved by the trial judge) to be available throughout the course of proceedings ☐ Supporting adult may sit with defendant at trial ☐ Defendant to sit near advocate rather than in the dock ☐ Defence to provide a note with any supporting material by Stage 2 providing all necessary welfare information to the court and as to the timetabling of the trial and regularity of breaks and any other measures required so that the defendant can maintain concentration to be reviewed by trial judge at a Ground Rules or other hearing pre-trial ☐ Wigs and robes not to be worn ☐ Dock security staff to wear civilian clothes ☐ Save for good reason there be no uniformed police presence in the courtroom; ☐ Trial to be conducted in adapted courtroom where participants are on the same or almost the same level ☐ Public/Press numbers attending the trial in the courtroom will be restricted and a video relay will be required ☐ Defendant to have pre-trial visit to allocated courtroom to be during non-sitting hours. (accompanied by intermediary if appointed) ☐ Trial to be conducted throughout, so far as possible, in clear language so that the defendant can understand the proceedings and evidence of witnesses, and in accordance with relevant Advocates Gateway Toolkits or the ICCA 20 Principles of Questioning ☐ Other:
Measures to assist the defendant to give evidence CrimPD V 18	If the defendant seeks additional special measures such as the use of live link (with or without pre-trial practice) or screens to give evidence, or to have a supporter (other than an

V2.9 (03/07/2019)

FORM - PTPH NG 2

	intermediary) in the live-link room or to sit near the defendant during evidence or other special measure then a formal application will be required at Stage 2
Has the Judge given an oral judgement on the measures required? ☑	☐ Yes ☐ No

Pleas	
Judicial checks and comments	☐ Confirmed which version of indictment being pursued if more than one ☐ Confirmed with prosecutor that indictment properly sets out the offences (CrimPR 3.24) ☐ Confirmed that defence advocate has explained the allegation(s) and has given advice on credit for plea ☐ Judge explained the allegation(s) and gave warning to defendant on credit for plea Comment:
Pleas entered at PTPH or reason if not arraigned	

Trial				
Date	*Listing*	*Time Estimate*	☑ *Facilities required*	Directions
	☐ Fixture ☐ Backer ☐ Fixed Floater ☐ Priority Floater ☐ Warned List commencing.	days weeks	☐ Live Link ☐ Satellite or UKLINK from: ☐ Interpreter for defendant(s) (language):	
Certificates of Readiness to be filed by all parties (If no date is inserted then to be 28 days before trial date)				
Orders made in respect of defendant(s) or charge(s) where there has been a guilty plea, but where a trial is still required (e.g. as to timing of or arrangements for sentence of co-defendants)				

Stage 1 - Unless individual dates are provided the prosecution shall serve the following by: Ordinarily 50 days (custody cases) or 70 days (bail cases) after sending.		**Date:**
Item	*Date*	*Additional requirements/particulars/directions if any*
Service of prosecution case to include making available ABE transcripts and recordings relied on		
Initial disclosure (if not yet served)		
Updated or initial Disclosure Management Document – to address issues raised by defence on the PTPH form		
Multi-media evidence (inc. CCTV and BWV) relied upon as part of the prosecution case		
Written record of defendant's taped interview(s) (ROTI). Unless otherwise ordered where there is a substantially "no		

V2.9 (03/07/2019)

FORM - PTPH NG 2

comment" interview a short summary rather than a full transcript is sufficient. In any event the parties are expected to engage pre-trial to agree a summary or editing.		
Audio recording of defendant's taped interviews(s) to be ordered only if the defendant cannot apply to the investigator for audio under PACE		
999 call transcript(s) and recording(s) if relied upon as part of the prosecution case		
Telephone, text or other social media records if relied on as part of the prosecution case [Generally, an individual date will need to be considered]		
Telephone, cell site, social media, and/or timeline analysis [Generally, an individual date will need to be considered]		
Forensic statements (SFR 2 or MG11) that can be served by Stage 1. This order only applies where, in relation to SFR1 (or other served summary of expert's conclusions), the defendant has identified on the PTPH form a conclusion that is not admitted and what the disputed issues are. The SFR2 or MG11 will be limited to those identified issues		
Bad character notice(s) with supporting evidence relied on CrimPR 21		
Hearsay application(s) CrimPR 20		
Special measures application(s) CrimPR 18		
Other:		

Third Party Disclosure: Unless individual dates are provided the prosecution shall serve the following by:	**Date:**
The following areas of third party material have been identified:	
Prosecution shall either make requests to third party and if necessary apply for third party disclosure summonses, OR notify defence in writing that no requests will be made for third party disclosure by	
If the prosecution is to pursue third party disclosure, then the prosecution must serve a report in writing on the outcome of efforts to identify potentially disclosable materials held by third parties and any ongoing enquiries not yet completed. The same may be included in a Disclosure Management Document by	
Any disclosable third party disclosure shall be served on the defence by	
Prosecution to make any application required to the Family Court by	
Other:	

Stage 2 - Unless individual dates are provided it is ordered that the defence shall serve the following by: Ordinarily 28 days after Stage 1		**Date:**
Item	*Date*	*Additional requirements/particulars/directions*
Defence Statement to include particulars of alibi; and requests for disclosure, describing the material and explaining, by reference to the issues in the case, why it is disclosable		

V2.9 (03/07/2019)

FORM - PTPH NG 2

Response to prosecution Disclosure Management Document if served identifying by reference to the issues in the case any disputes as to reasonable lines of enquiry or levels of data extraction		
Standard Witness Table of prosecution witnesses required to give live evidence; defence witnesses and interpreter requirements		
Response to Summary of Expert Conclusions (SFR1) stating which, if any, of the expert's conclusions are admitted as fact and where a conclusion is not admitted stating what are the disputed issues concerning that conclusion. A defendant who did not identify such issues on the PTPH form and does not serve such a response is taken to admit as fact the conclusions of the summary (SFR1).		
Response to prosecution bad character notice(s) - CrimPR 21		
Response to prosecution hearsay application(s) - CrimPR 20		
Response to prosecution special measures application(s) - CrimPR 18		
Special measures application for defendant or defence witnesses. Any reply from prosecution or other party to be served within 14 days		
Defence expert evidence to be relied upon - CrimPR 19		
Other:		

Stage 3 – Unless individual dates are provided it is ordered that the prosecution shall serve the following by: Ordinarily 14 or 28 days after Stage 2		**Date:**
Item	*Date*	*Additional requirements/particulars/directions*
Further disclosure of items required to be disclosed under CPIA resulting from or requested by the Defence Statement. (If the Defence Statement is served late the prosecution have a like period from service of the Defence Statement as between Stages 2 and 3 to serve further disclosure)		
Further updated Disclosure Management Document. (If the Defence DMD response is served late the prosecution have a like period from service of the DMD Response as between Stages 2 and 3 to serve further disclosure)		
Further evidence to be relied upon that could not be served by Stage 1		
Forensic science statements (SFR2 or MG11) required as a result of the Defence response to a summary of conclusions (SFR1) - CrimPR 19.3		
Expert medical evidence		
Psychiatric evidence		
Other (specify) expert evidence		
Satellite/UKLINK/Live link application(s). CrimPD 18.23-24		

V2.9 (03/07/2019)

FORM - PTPH NG 2

Intermediary report(s) with draft specific Ground Rules if to be applied for. CrimPR 18 & 3.9(7)		For Witness:
List of editing proposals to ABE interview recording		
Other:		

Stage 4 – Unless individual dates are given it is ordered that the defence shall serve the following by: Ordinarily 14 or 28 days after Stage 3		**Date:**
Item	*Date*	*Additional requirements/particulars/directions*
Complaint about prosecution non-disclosure to comply with s.8 CPIA and CrimPR 15.5		
Application(s) for witness summons for third party disclosure if the prosecution indicates at PTPH that it will not be pursuing any TPD issues OR any defendant is dissatisfied with the outcome of prosecution enquiries		
List of editing proposals to ABE interview recording (if any) and response to prosecution proposals (if served)		
s.100 or 101 bad character of non-defendant application - CrimPR 21. Any reply from prosecution or other party to be served within 14 days		
S.41 Evidence of sexual behaviour application - CrimPR 22 and CrimPD V 22A - Any reply from prosecution or other party to be served within 14 days		
Response to prosecution intermediary report(s) - CrimPR 18		
Intermediary report for defendant or defence witnesses with draft ground rules. Any reply from prosecution or other party to be served within 14 days		
Satellite/UKLINK/Live link application(s) CrimPD 18.23-24		
Defence expert evidence to be relied upon that could not be served by Stage 2 - CrimPR 19		
Other:		

Pre-Arraignment FCMH - Abuse; Dismissal; Severance; Other			
To resolve	*Date*	⏱ *Time Estimate*	*Directions*
☐ Abuse of Process ☐ Dismissal application ☐ Joinder/Severance ☐ Other issue:		minutes hours	☐ Defendant not required ☐ Defendant must attend ☐ Suitable for PVL ☐ Other:
☐ Application/skeleton and supporting materials by:			
☐ Response and supporting materials by:			

Pre-Arraignment FCMH - Fitness to participate in the trial process			
To resolve	*Date*	⏱ *Time Estimate*	*Directions*
☐ Fitness to participate in the trial process		minutes	☐ Defendant not required

V2.9 (03/07/2019)

FORM - PTPH NG 2

☐ Other issue:		hours	☐ Defendant must attend ☐ Suitable for PVL or Hospital Link ☐ Other:

Where the Court has a Mental Health Liaison and Diversion Service the Defence must engage with the service
☐ Defence first medical report (or notice to the court and prosecution in writing that defendant is fit and the case should be listed for arraignment) by:
☐ Prosecution to notify defence if the prosecution do OR do not intend to obtain medical report within 7 days or by:
☐ If prosecution are to serve medical report then to be served by:
☐ If prosecution are not to serve medical report then defence to serve any second medical report by:

Pre-Trial Recorded Cross-Examination (s.28) – Vulnerable Witnesses – s.16 YJCEA

The judge being satisfied that the following witness(es) is/are eligible for assistance under s.16 of the YJCEA a s.28 direction is made that their ABE interviews shall stand as their evidence in chief and they shall be cross examined in advance of the trial

Witness		Date of Birth	
Witness		Date of Birth	
Witness		Date of Birth	

The case is allocated to [Judge]:
The future management of the case will be under the supervision of the trial judge

s.4 Contempt of Court Act 1981 order has been made for ☐ the Ground Rules Hearing ☐ s.28 hearing

Timetable

Item	*Date*	*Time Marking*	*☑ Directions*	*Time Estimate*
Intermediary report(s) to be served by:				
Ground Rules Form and any applications relevant to the witness – eg s.100 bad character; s.41 sexual behaviour; or s.8 non-disclosure to be served by				
Responses to above applications to be served by				
s.28 directions and Ground Rules Hearing			☐ Defendant not required ☐ Defendant must attend ☐ Suitable for PVL Any intermediary relied on shall attend the Ground Rules Hearing	minutes hours
Date for witness to refresh their memory			The officer in the case or another suitable police officer (or investigator equivalent) shall attend during the memory refreshing and make a note of any material comment by the witness	

V2.9 (03/07/2019)

FORM - PTPH NG 2

The judge and advocates shall meet the witness on			The advocates are not to meet the witness without the judge	minutes hours
Pre-trial cross-examination Hearing			Defendant to attend in person Any intermediary relied on shall attend the Examination Hearing. Attendance of witness to be timetabled	minutes hours
Supplemental Special Measures Orders:				
Supplemental Orders:				

Pre-Trial Recorded Cross-Examination (s.28) – Intimidated Witnesses – s.17 YJCEA				
The judge being satisfied that the following witness(es) is/are eligible for assistance under s.17 of the YJCEA a s.28 direction is made that their ABE interviews shall stand as their evidence in chief and they shall be cross examined in advance of the trial				
Witness			Date of Birth if u.18	
Witness			Date of Birth if u.18	
Witness			Date of Birth if u.18	
The case is allocated to [Judge]: The future management of the case will be under the supervision of the trial judge				
s.4 Contempt of Court Act 1981 order has been made for ☐ the Ground Rules Hearing ☐ s.28 hearing				
Timetable				
Item	*Date*	*Time Marking*	☑ *Directions*	⏲ *Time Estimate*
Applications relevant to the witness – eg s.100 bad character; s.41 sexual behaviour; s.8 non-disclosure to be served by				
Responses to above applications to be served by				
s.28 directions hearing The hearing may be vacated on <u>all</u> parties informing the Court CPO in writing that they are fully ready and no orders are required			☐ Defendant not required ☐ Defendant must attend ☐ Suitable for PVL	minutes hours
Date for witness to refresh their memory			The officer in the case or another suitable police officer (or investigator equivalent) shall attend during the memory refreshing and make a note of any material comment by the witness	
Pre-trial cross-examination Hearing			Defendant to attend in person. Attendance of witness to be timetabled	minutes hours
Supplemental Special Measures directions:				
Supplemental Orders:				

V2.9 (03/07/2019)

FORM - PTPH NG 2

FCMH - General			
To resolve	*Date*	⏱ *Time Estimate*	☑ *Directions*
		minutes hours	☐ Defendant not required ☐ Defendant must attend ☐ Suitable for PVL ☐ Application/skeleton and supporting materials by: ☐ Response and supporting materials by:

Pre-Trial Review - General			
	Date	⏱ *Time Estimate*	☑ *Directions*
The PTR may be vacated on <u>all</u> parties informing the court CPO in writing by Certificates of Readiness that they are fully trial ready and no orders are required. Specific issues to be considered:		minutes hours	☐ Defendant not required ☐ Defendant must attend ☐ Suitable for PVL ☐ Other:

Ground Rules and Welfare and/or S.41 Sexual Behaviour and Pre-Trial Review – (not s.28)			
	Date	⏱ *Time Estimate*	☑ *Directions*
Specific issues to be considered:		minutes hours	☐ GRH for prosecution witnesses ☐ GRH for defendant or defence witnesses ☐ Hearing to determine s.41 Sexual Behaviour application ☐ Defendant not required ☐ Defendant must attend ☐ Suitable for PVL Any intermediary relied on to attend. ☐ Not an intermediary case ☐ Other:

Trial Preparation **(these orders will only be required in more substantial cases)**			
Prosecution	*Date*	*Defence*	*Date*
Opening Note Draft agreed facts (admissions) Draft jury bundle index		Notice of objections; comments; responses, and requests for inclusion	
Prosecution draft edited defendant's interview (ROTI)		Defence response to defendant's interview edits	
Witness Timetable for prosecution witnesses with copy to the Witness Service		Any defence response to Witness Timetable	
Other:		Other:	

V2.9 (03/07/2019)

FORM - PTPH NG 2

Standard Orders for Witnesses and Defendant	
Video Links	1. Where a defendant appears at PTPH by video link from custody without objection at the hearing the court makes a live link direction under s.57B Crime and Disorder Act 1998
Witness requirements	2. The witness requirements are as confirmed by the court on the Witness List and any special measures or orders endorsed shall apply
	3. If no Standard Witness Table is served by a defendant, the served written statements of witnesses (compliant with s.9 CJA 1967 and with notice as required by CrimPR 16) not listed as required in the Witness Table at PTPH shall be admissible as evidence to the like extent as oral evidence to the like effect by that witness
Where Special measures are granted for the use of ABE interviews; live link or screens	4. Where a witness has provided an ABE interview, the ABE interview as edited by agreement or by order of the court shall stand as that witness' evidence in chief unless otherwise ordered
	5. A witness whose ABE interview is relied on shall view that interview in the week preceding the trial in the presence of the officer in the case (or equivalent) or other suitable police officer (or investigator equivalent) who shall record any material comment the witness shall make and pass that record to the prosecutor
	6. Any preference between screens or live link shall be identified after a court visit and shall include the witness' reasons for the preference
	7. The attendance of any such witness at trial must be timetabled for the time when the witness is expected to commence examination
Young or vulnerable witnesses or defendants CrimPR 18 & 3.9(7)	8. Young or vulnerable witnesses or defendants to whom an Advocates Gateway Toolkit or the ICCA 20 Principles of Questioning apply are to be examined and cross-examined in accordance with those principles unless those are superseded by specific ground rules
Where provision is made for a witness by UKLINK or SAT	9. Particulars of the link must be provided not less than three weeks before trial - CrimPD 18.23-4
Expert witnesses – CrimPR 19	10. Expert witnesses of comparable disciplines must liaise and serve on the parties and the Court a statement of the points on which they agree and disagree with reasons no less than 14 days prior to the trial OR by such date as may be inserted here:

Additional Orders:	
Additional Order	*Date*

Final Judicial Warnings:	
Judicial warnings given ☑	☐ That failure to provide a sufficiently detailed Defence Statement may count against the defendant
	☐ That failure to attend when required, whether from custody or bail, may be a separate offence
	☐ At trial the defendant will have the right to give evidence
	☐ If the defendant fails to attend trial the trial may proceed in his/her absence in which case advocates may withdraw and the judge may inform the jury of the reason for that absence
	Other:
Judicial warnings not given ☑	☐ Reason:

V2.9 (03/07/2019)

CHAPTER FOUR

DEFENCE STATEMENTS AND WITNESS NOTICES

This chapter sets out the law and guidance in relation to the service of defence statements. We also look at the topic of defence witness notices which are often served at the same time. There are prescribed forms to use for defence statements and defence witness notices, which can be found on the justice.gov.uk website. Click on 'Procedure rules', 'Criminal procedure rules', 'Criminal Procedure Rules: Forms' then 'Disclosure'. Copies of these forms are also set out at the end of this chapter.

Compulsory disclosure by the accused

Section 5(5) of the CPIA provides that an accused **must** give a defence statement to the court and the prosecutor in Crown Court cases. This obligation applies where, *"the prosecutor complies with section 3 or purports to comply with it"* (section 5(1)(b)).

Voluntary disclosure by the accused

Section 6 of the CPIA, provides that service of a defence statement is not mandatory in magistrates' court proceedings. However, there are advantages of serving a defence statement, even where one is not required. Practically, it prompts the prosecution to engage with their disclosure obligations by reviewing the unused material and addressing specific points in advance of the trial. In addition, a section 8 application cannot be made unless a defence statement has been served.

So, although a defence statement is not mandatory in the magistrates' court, serving one adds an important weapon in the defence's armoury, namely the ability to make a section 8 application.

Section 8 applications are examined further in **Chapter Five**.

Contents of a defence statement

The material parts of section 6A of the CPIA are as follows,

> "**6A Contents of defence statement**
>
> *(1) For the purposes of this Part a defence statement is a written statement—*
>
> > *(a) setting out the nature of the accused's defence, including any particular defences on which he intends to rely,*
> >
> > *(b) indicating the matters of fact on which he takes issue with the prosecution,*
> >
> > *(c) setting out, in the case of each such matter, why he takes issue with the prosecution,*
> >
> > *(ca) setting out particulars of the matters of fact on which he intends to rely for the purposes of his defence,*
> >
> > *(d) indicating any point of law (including any point as to the admissibility of evidence or an abuse of process) which he wishes to take, and any authority on which he intends to rely for that purpose.*
>
> *(2) A defence statement that discloses an alibi must give particulars of it, including—*
>
> > *(a) the name, address and date of birth of any witness the accused believes is able to give evidence in support of the alibi, or as many*

of those details as are known to the accused when the statement is given;

(b) any information in the accused's possession which might be of material assistance in identifying or finding any such witness in whose case any of the details mentioned in paragraph (a) are not known to the accused when the statement is given.

(3) For the purposes of this section evidence in support of an alibi is evidence tending to show that by reason of the presence of the accused at a particular place or in a particular area at a particular time he was not, or was unlikely to have been, at the place where the offence is alleged to have been committed at the time of its alleged commission.

…"

It is worth noting paragraph 34 of the Court of Appeal decision in *Re Joseph Hill & Co, Solicitors* [2014] 1WLR 786, which states that,

"The statutory obligation to give the name and address of an alibi is triggered by the defendant's belief that the witness is able to give evidence in support of the alibi. It is not necessary that the alibi witness can give such evidence let alone that he or she is also willing to do so. Nor is the defendant's belief in the witness's ability to give evidence dependent on the witness giving a proof of evidence; if it were, the efficacy of this provision would be easily defeated by the failure of the witness to co-operate."

There is, of course, a natural tendency for the defendant to want to keep their powder dry, before seeing how the evidence develops. However, a skeletal defence statement is unlikely to identify the real disclosure issues. It is highly likely to be deemed inadequate by the Prosecution. Achieving the balance of a detailed defence statement which triggers disclosure, whilst bearing in mind that the defence statement can be used by the prosecution as a weapon in cross-examination of the defendant and in certain circumstances may even be provided to the jury, requires judgement, focus and attention to detail in the drafting of this crucial document.

The particulars of a defence statement, although drafted by practitioners, are actually attributable to the defendant. Therefore, it is imperative to seek to ensure that the contents of the defence statement have been verified by the client and signed before service of the document on the prosecution.

The real advantage to the defence in providing an adequately detailed defence statement is that it places an obligation upon the prosecution to review the unused material to establish whether in light of the defence statement, there is any material that may reasonably be considered capable of undermining the prosecution case or of assisting the defence case.

Material disclosed after service of the defence statement must be reviewed with great care, as this is usually where the arising disclosure issues can be identified.

In the event that unforeseen disclosure issues arise in the course of the trial, an adequately detailed defence statement can be deployed and referred to by the defence to assert that these were live issues identified by the defence at the outset of the trial.

Defence Witness Notices

In addition to providing details of an alibi witness in the defence statement, the defence must also provide information to the prosecution about any other witness they intend to call. Section 6C of the CPIA provides that,

> "**6C Notification of intention to call defence witnesses**

(1) The accused must give to the court and the prosecutor a notice indicating whether he intends to call any persons (other than himself) as witnesses at his trial and, if so—

(a) giving the name, address and date of birth of each such proposed witness, or as many of those details as are known to the accused when the notice is given;

(b) providing any information in the accused's possession which might be of material assistance in identifying or finding any such proposed witness in whose case any of the details mentioned in paragraph (a) are not known to the accused when the notice is given.

(2) Details do not have to be given under this section to the extent that they have already been given under section 6A(2).

(3) The accused must give a notice under this section during the period which, by virtue of section 12, is the relevant period for this section.

(4) If, following the giving of a notice under this section, the accused—

(a) decides to call a person (other than himself) who is not included in the notice as a proposed witness, or decides not to call a person who is so included, or

(b) discovers any information which, under subsection (1), he would have had to include in the notice if he had been aware of it when giving the notice,

he must give an appropriately amended notice to the court and the prosecutor."

A copy of the Defence Witness Notice form is set out at the end of this chapter.

Time limits for service of defence statements and defence witness notices

In a Crown Court case, the time limit for service of a defence statement and any defence witness notice is **28 days** after initial disclosure (or notice from the prosecutor that there is no material to disclose). In other words, within 28 days of receiving the prosecution's section 3 letter. In magistrates' court cases, the time limit is **14 days.**

Criminal Procedure and Investigations Act 1996 (Defence Disclosure Time Limits) Regulations 2011

The Regulations provides as follows:

> "2. — ***Prescribed period for disclosure by the accused***
>
> *(1) The relevant period for section 5 (compulsory disclosure), section 6 (voluntary disclosure) and section 6C (notification of intention to call defence witnesses) begins with the day on which the prosecutor complies or purports to comply with section 3 (initial duty of the prosecutor to disclose).*
>
> *(2) In a case where Part 1 applies by virtue of section 1(1) (application of Part 1 in respect of summary proceedings), the relevant period for section 6 and section 6C expires at the end of 14 days beginning with the first day of the relevant period.*
>
> *(3) In a case where Part 1 applies by virtue of section 1(2) (application of Part 1 in respect of Crown Court proceedings), the relevant period for section 5 and section 6C expires at the end of 28 days beginning with the first day of the relevant period.*
>
> *(4) Where the relevant period would expire on a Saturday, Sunday, Christmas Day, Good Friday or any day that under the Banking and Financial Dealings Act 1971 is a bank holiday in*

England and Wales, the relevant period is treated as expiring on the next day that is not one of those days.

(5) Paragraphs (2) and (3) are subject to regulation 3.

3.— Power to extend

(1) The court may by order extend (or further extend) the relevant period by so many days as it specifies.

(2) The court may only make such an order—

(a) on an application by the accused; and

(b) if it is satisfied that it would be unreasonable to require the accused to give a defence statement under section 5 or section 6, or give notice under section 6C, as the case may be, within the relevant period.

(3) Such an application must—

(a) be made within the relevant period;

(b) specify the grounds on which it is made; and

(c) state the number of days by which the accused wishes the relevant period to be extended.

(4) There is no limit on the number of applications that may be made under paragraph (2)(a)."

If the volume of the unused is too lengthy or there are outstanding issues about the contents and or detail of the defence statement, then it would be advisable to seek a written extension of the 28 days.

This will avoid the client facing an adverse inference from late service and allows the whole defence team to be satisfied that the document served meets the criteria which should prompt a considered response form the prosecution.

It is important to bear in mind the wording of regulation 3(3)(a), namely that an application to extend must be made **within** the relevant period, not after it has expired. Therefore, making a note of stage dates in professional diaries assists to ensure compliance with court directions.

The defence are ordinarily ordered to serve the defence statement by the Stage 2 date, which is set at the PTPH, and is usually 28 days after Stage 1. Please see PTPH form at the end of **Chapter Three**.

Although the service of a defence statement falls to be considered under Stage 2, the PTPH form allows for an alternative date to be inserted, specifically in relation to the service of defence statements. This is worth bearing in mind at the PTPH. It may be necessary to ask for additional time to serve a defence statement if there are reasons why 28 days would be insufficient.

Signatures

A defence statement should be verified and signed. However, note the wording of section 6E(1) of the CPIA, which states that,

> *"Where an accused's solicitor purports to give on behalf of the accused-*
>
> *(a) a defence statement...*
>
> *The statement shall, unless the contrary is proved, be deemed to be given with the authority of the accused."*

Prosecution claims that the defence statement is inadequate

If, when prosecuting a case, it is unclear from the defence statement what the defence is and what matters are actually in dispute, it then becomes difficult to judge whether unused material passes the disclosure test or not. In such circumstances, the defence should be asked to provide an adequate defence statement. The inadequacy of the defence statement can also be brought to the court's attention, with a view to inviting the judge to set a timetable for the defence to provide a supplementary defence statement setting out more clearly what their defence is and when the prosecution should respond to that further defence statement by.

Paragraph 125 of the Attorney General's Guidelines on Disclosure (2022) gives an indication of what may be considered to be an inadequate defence statement:

"125. Defence practitioners must ensure that defence statements are drafted in accordance with the requirements in the CPIA 1996. Defence statements must not make general and unspecified allegations in order to seek far reaching disclosure and should not describe the defence in ambiguous or limited terms (such as self-defence, mistaken identity, consent)."

Proactively challenging the adequacy of defence statements appears to be encouraged by paragraph 126 of the Attorney General's Guidelines on Disclosure (2022), which states:

"126. It is vital that prosecutors consider defence statements thoroughly. Prosecutors should challenge the lack of (in the Crown Court) or inadequate defence statements in writing, copying the document to the court and the defence and seeking directions from the court to require the provision of an adequate defence statement from the defence as soon as possible."

Supplementary defence statements

There is no power for a judge to force the defence to provide a supplementary defence statement. When defending, and faced with a prosecution claim that the defence statement is inadequate, carefully consider whether this claim is justified. Analyse whether the defence statement is too sparse and unclear to be able to properly trigger the disclosure that may help the client. Whatever conclusion you reach, either to provide a supplementary defence statement or not, it would be sensible to first advise the client of the consequences, such as the risk of an adverse inference being drawn, and to obtain an endorsement. Adverse inferences are considered later in this chapter.

Supplementary defence statements are an under-deployed tool that can be used by the defence to focus the disclosure exercise.

In addition to a supplementary defence statement being prompted by the prosecution claiming that the original defence statement is inadequate, there are two other scenarios in which those who defend may wish to consider serving such a document.

First, this may come about if the client changes his position or provides instructions for the first time in relation to an aspect of the case that you consider to be important.

Second, an issue may arise (or occur to you) during preparation for or even during the trial itself. You may, for example, consider that a particular issue is now live, whereas it was not previously flagged up as being controversial. It may be helpful in these circumstances to provide a supplementary defence statement on this issue accompanied by, if appropriate, a section 8 application.

Simply making a section 8 application without providing a supplementary defence statement may result in the judge refusing the application on the basis that the issue was not even raised in the original defence statement. A supplementary defence statement need not be a lengthy document and could, as a bare minimum for example, state that having considered specific material, the evidence of witness X is now in issue.

Disclosing defence statements of co-defendants

The Court of Appeal in *R v Cairns* [2002] EWCA Crim 2838 stated, at paragraph 78,

> *"...But if the prosecutor, having received the defence statements of co-defendants, forms the view that a defence statement of one might reasonably be expected to assist the defence of another defendant, then in those circumstances the obligation under section 7 to make secondary disclosure would cover that defence statement.*
>
> *We emphasise that that does not mean automatic disclosure of defence statements by the Crown in all cases where more than one defendant is being tried. The Crown has to make the usual judgment under section 7(2) of the 1996 Act. But if the terms of that subsection are met, such defence statements should be disclosed, subject of course to any issue as to public interest immunity which may arise."*

Although *Cairns* refers to the old secondary disclosure stage, the Court of Appeal's dicta is still applicable to current cases. In short, if a defence statement passes the disclosure test, it should be disclosed.

A good example is if defendants are each running a cut-throat defence. Defendant A and B might blame each other as to who attacked the victim. If defendant A had earlier provided a defence statement setting out a different defence, for example alibi, that defence statement should be disclosed. Defendant A's defence statement could assist defendant B as defendant B's advocate could cross-examine defendant A on his defence statement and, with the court's permission, make adverse comment about it pursuant to section 11(5) of the CPIA, which is considered below.

Use of defence statements in evidence

In appropriate cases, the prosecution may seek to place the defence statement, or at least extracts of it, before the jury as evidence. Again, to use the example of a case where the defence statement sets out an alibi defence, but then the defence at trial changes to self-defence, the prosecution may seek to place the defence statement before the jury.

The relevant parts of section 6E of the *CPIA 1996* provide as follows:

"...(4) The judge in a trial before a judge and jury –

(a) may direct that the jury be given a copy of any defence statement, and

(b) if he does so, may direct that it be edited so as not to include references to matters evidence of which would be inadmissible.

(5) A direction under subsection (4) –

(a) may be made either of the judge's own motion or on the application of any party;

(b) may be made only if the judge is of the opinion that seeing a copy of the defence statement would help the jury to understand the case or to resolve any issue in the case."

In *R v Sanghera and Takhar* [2012] 2 Cr App R 17, the Court of Appeal held that in accordance with s.6E(5)(b) of the CPIA, a judge could only make an order directing that the jury be given a copy of a defence statement if he was of the opinion that seeing a copy of the defence statement would help the jury to understand the case or to resolve any issue in the case. Accordingly, the judge had to form an opinion as to whether the defence statement would help the jury. The judge also had to exercise a judgment as to whether, overall, he should make the direction sought, and he might also have to exercise a judgment as to when and on what terms the defence statement was to be put before the jury.

Adverse comment and other consequences of inadequate or late defence statements and defence witness notices

At the PTPH, the judge will invariably warn the defendant that failure to provide a sufficiently detailed defence statement may count against him.

Failure to provide a defence statement at all will also deprive the defence of the ability to make a section 8 application.

Failure to provide an adequate defence statement will also affect the consequent ongoing disclosure that is provided by the prosecution as a result of the issues, or lack of issues, identified by the defence in this document.

It is also important to bear in mind that a defendant may be cross-examined on his defence statement.

On occasion, a client may claim, under cross-examination, that their defence statement does not reflect what they told their solicitor, or that they had not verified its contents. When defending, to help avoid this situation from arising, it is best practice to insist, as a matter of priority, that the contents of the document are verified, signed and dated. If this step has been omitted, there is a danger that the issue of privilege is then raised and the client will need to be advised on whether they wish to waive legal professional privilege.

Section 11 of the CPIA sets out the potential consequences for disclosure failures by the defence.

> ***"11.— Faults in disclosure by accused.***
>
> *(1) This section applies in the three cases set out in subsections (2), (3) and (4).*
>
> *(2) The first case is where section 5 applies and the accused—*
>
> > *(a) fails to give an initial defence statement,*
> >
> > *(b) gives an initial defence statement but does so after the end of the period which, by virtue of section 12, is the relevant period for section 5…,*
> >
> > *(e) sets out inconsistent defences in his defence statement, or*

(f) at his trial—

(i) puts forward a defence which was not mentioned in his defence statement or is different from any defence set out in that statement,

(ii) relies on a matter (or any particular of any matter of fact) which, in breach of the requirements imposed by or under section 6A, was not mentioned in his defence statement,

(iii) adduces evidence in support of an alibi without having given particulars of the alibi in his defence statement, or

(iv) calls a witness to give evidence in support of an alibi without having complied with section 6A(2)(a) or (b) as regards the witness in his defence statement.

(3) The second case is where section 6 applies, the accused gives an initial defence statement, and the accused—

(a) gives the initial defence statement after the end of the period which, by virtue of section 12, is the relevant period for section 6,

or

(b) does any of the things mentioned in paragraphs (c) to (f) of subsection (2).

(4) The third case is where the accused—

(a) gives a witness notice but does so after the end of the period which, by virtue of section 12, is the relevant period for section 6C, or

(b) at his trial calls a witness (other than himself) not included, or not adequately identified, in a witness notice.

(5) Where this section applies—

(a) the court or any other party may make such comment as appears appropriate;

(b) the court or jury may draw such inferences as appear proper in deciding whether the accused is guilty of the offence concerned.

(6) Where—

(a) this section applies by virtue of subsection (2)(f)(ii) (including that provision as it applies by virtue of subsection (3)(b)), and

(b) the matter which was not mentioned is a point of law (including any point as to the admissibility of evidence or an abuse of process) or an authority,

comment by another party under subsection (5)(a) may be made only with the leave of the court.

(7) Where this section applies by virtue of subsection (4), comment by another party under subsection (5)(a) may be made only with the leave of the court.

(8) Where the accused puts forward a defence which is different from any defence set out in his defence statement, in doing anything under subsection (5) or in deciding whether to do anything under it the court shall have regard—

(a) to the extent of the differences in the defences, and

(b) to whether there is any justification for it.

(9) Where the accused calls a witness whom he has failed to include, or to identify adequately, in a witness notice, in doing anything under subsection (5) or in deciding whether to do anything under it the court shall have regard to whether there is any justification for the failure.

(10) A person shall not be convicted of an offence solely on an inference drawn under subsection (5)…"

In *R v Essa* [2009] EWCA 43, the Court of Appeal provided the following helpful analysis on the approach to adverse comment on a defendant's failure to mention a fact in, or to even provide, a defence statement,

"21. The complaint … is that the judge did not tell the jury that the absence of the defence statement was because of advice. We agree that if that advice had been in evidence, the judge should certainly have dealt with and with its significance in a way no doubt roughly analogous to the way in which legal advice is dealt with in a section 34 direction. But the short answer to the potential submission is that it was not in evidence. The opportunity to put it in evidence had undoubtedly been there, and no doubt it would not have been contested if it had been asserted, but it was not. In those circumstances the application for leave to appeal in relation to the direction upon the absence of the defence statement cannot succeed.

22. We should we think add that, just as in a case in which section 34 is engaged a measure of judgment is wise as to whether it really advances the case significantly or not, the same applies to the absence of a defence statement in a case in which, as it emerges at trial, no positive defence is advanced and merely an assertion is made that the appellant was not there. In such circumstances the absence of the defence statement is not of zero significance; it is capable of leading to the conclusion that the appellant wished to keep all his options open and that because he was guilty. But in such a case its significance may well be marginal and once again a degree of judgment is advisable in the decision both whether to embark upon cross-examination about it and, if cross-examination is embarked upon, the terms in which a direction be given.

23. Lastly, we should deal with the argument… to the effect that section 11(5) of the Criminal Procedure and Investigations Act is

incompatible with the right to a fair trial enshrined in Article 6 of the European Convention on Human Rights. Certain it is that the right to silence is part of the right to a fair trial, as it is certain, even more importantly but distinctly, that the right not to incriminate oneself is. Those two rights are different. However, for the same reasons as section 34 is compatible with the European Convention, so is section 11(5) which entitles comment by the Crown on the absence of a defence statement. Contrary to any submission otherwise, the use which can be made of section 11(5) is not without judicial control. True it is that the Crown does not now need to make a preliminary application to the judge for leave to cross-examine upon the topic. That does not prevent the judge from interfering and stopping the cross-examination if it is unfair, still less does it avoid the necessity for the judge to decide, if such cross-examination has been embarked upon, the terms in which he directs the jury. If the cross-examination was unfair it is open to the judge to tell the judge to disregard it. In those circumstances, there is no doubt that section 11(5) is perfectly compatible with the Convention."

Interaction with section 34 directions

At paragraph 44 of Lord Justice Gross and Lord Justice Treacy's 'Further Review of Disclosure in Criminal Proceedings: sanctions for disclosure failure' (November 2012), the following analysis was provided in relation to the interaction between section 11 of the CPIA and section 34 of the *Criminal Justice and Public Order Act* 1994, the latter section dealing with the effect of an accused's failure to mention facts when questioned or charged:

"If there has also been a defence failure to mention a fact in interview in addition to a failure of disclosure under section 11(2), the judge will need to consider whether to use section 11 of CPIA 1996 or whether to give a direction under section 34 of the Criminal Justice and Public Order Act 1994; it will rarely be appropriate for two such directions to be given. Since the defence statement is due to be provided considerably later in the criminal process than the interview takes

place, after the prosecution evidence and initial disclosure has been served, the inference under section 11 might be thought to be stronger than the inference under section 34 and therefore section 11 might be used in preference. Section 11(8) sets out matters to which the court must have regard before exercising the powers under subsection 5."

R v Haynes

A useful authority when addressing the court on how and indeed whether to direct a jury in relation to inconsistencies between a defence run at trial and that set out in a defence statement, is the Court of Appeal decision in *R v Haynes* [2012] EWCA Crim 3281. Moses LJ (as he then was), gave the following guidance at paragraphs 9 and 10:

"9. Cases such as this where there are discrepancies between the defence statement and the evidence are however less acute. The Crown Court Bench Book of March 2010 suggests at page 274, paragraph 16, that if there are discrepancies then directions as to legitimate inferences will be similar to those required for section 34 of the Criminal Justice and Public Order Act 1994 . But it is necessary yet again to emphasise that there must be flexibility in the way a jury is directed if the directions are to have any meaning at all. In this case it would have been meaningless to tell the jury that they cannot draw an adverse inference as to the defendant's credibility unless there is some evidence against him. It would have been meaningless to tell them that they cannot rely merely upon those discrepancies in order to convict in a case where there was plainly evidence against him… In those circumstances, the judge ought to have directed the jury at most that they should not draw any adverse inference as to the discrepancies unless they were sure that that statement was his statement. Since he had failed to call any evidence to explain what those details were doing [in] his defence statement, apart from merely saying "I had not seen it" that would not have particularly availed him. But some warning ought to have been given that they were not bound to draw an inference against him and that at most it probably went to his credibility and that anyway people accused of offences are liable to embellish things when they come to give their

evidence in order to make things look rather better than they otherwise appear.

10. So the lesson to be drawn from this case is that the judge was wrong not to discuss it in advance and wrong not to make it clear what decision he has reached as to whether adverse inferences should be drawn and then make some comment, which need only to have been short, to warn the jury not to jump to conclusions as a result of the difference. But we emphasise again…that questions and discussions as to a defence case statement are likely to fall well over the jury's head. … In short, lengthy directions slavishly following line by line the directions appropriate to section 34 of the Criminal Justice and Public Order Act would be only likely to deflect them from the task they had of deciding who was telling the truth and who was not."

In conclusion, whether prosecuting or defending, one of the key documents in the disclosure exercise is the defence statement. When turning your mind to how this document should be deployed and responded to, you may be assisted by the following checklist of questions:

DEFENCE STATEMENT CHECKLIST

- When is the deadline for service of the defence statement?
- Is it necessary to seek an extension of time to serve the defence statement?
- Has a defence statement already been served?
- Has it been signed and dated?
- Has a written record been kept to confirm that the client has verified the contents prior to signing?

- Have the prosecution responded in writing to the defence statement setting out whether or not further disclosure arises?
- Is there a need to provide a supplementary defence statement?
- Does the extent of the differences between the defence advanced at trial and the content of the defence statement warrant an adverse inference?
- Does the defendant have a justification for not including something in his defence statement?
- Has discussion taken place as to how the jury should be directed in relation to adverse inferences to be drawn from a failure to mention something in the defence statement?
- If an adverse inference direction is to be given, has consideration been given to whether a section 34 direction is now no longer required?

Template Defence Statement

IN THE … CROWN COURT Case No. …

REX

- v -

…

DEFENCE STATEMENT

To the Prosecutor: … Crown Prosecution Service

To the Court: … Crown Court

Defence Solicitors: …

Defence Counsel: …

Purpose: This statement is served in accordance with the provisions of Section 5 of the Criminal Procedure and Investigation Act 1996 and for no other purpose.

Confidentiality: This document is strictly confidential and is served only for the purpose to which it relates. It may not be used, wholly or in part, for any other purposes or in any other proceedings. It may not be disclosed to any persons other than a proper Officer of the Court, the Prosecution and the Disclosure Officer, without the prior written consent of the Defendant given through the solicitors for the defence.

Evidence/Disclosure: This Defence Statement is wholly reliant on the Prosecution's disclosure to the Defendant and his interpretation

of the same. This Defence Statement is without prejudice to the Defendant's right to seek to exclude at trial any evidence that may be referred to herein. The Defendant does not accept that any facts admitted are relevant, or that he has the means or knowledge to be satisfied that such admitted facts are true. The Defendant reserves the right not to rely upon such part(s) of this statement as relate to evidence that is not called by the Prosecution at trial, or is determined by the Court to be inadmissible. The Defendant reserves the right to serve a further and/or amended Defence Statement in the light of any further evidence (whether or not previously disclosed) and/or disclosure

The Defendant faces trial on a … count indictment alleging … , the particulars of which are as follows: …

Section 6A(1)(a): Nature of defence

The following sets out the particular of the defence: …

Section 6A(1)(b): Matters in Dispute

The primary matters in dispute in this case are: …

Section 6A(1)(c): Reasons why in dispute

Save where it is not evident from the matters set out herein, the Defendant takes issue with the Crown's evidence because there exists a material dispute as to fact and/or the manner in which the Crown's witnesses allege that the Defendant acted and/or the events that occurred. The Defendant reserves the right to take further, and alternative, issue with any Crown witness subject to what is said in oral evidence.

Section 6A(1)(ca): Facts relied on

The following sets out the particulars of the matters of fact on which the Defendant intends to rely for the purposes of his defence: …

Section 6A(1)(d): Issues of law

The Defendant identifies the following issues of law arising out of the prosecution papers served to-date:

...

The defence reserves the right to raise further issues of law in relation to matters which emerge from further consideration of the evidence in the case, further prosecution applications or out of any further disclosure.

The defence further reserves the right to raise objection to the admissibility of specific items of evidence once the Crown have identified the proposed contents of the jury bundle.

Section 7A: Continuing duty of prosecutor to disclose

Pursuant to those matters outlined herein, the Defendant believes that the following material (inter alia) might reasonably be considered capable of undermining the case for the prosecution against the Defendant or of assisting the defence as disclosed above and, therefore, should be disclosed pursuant to section 7A:

...

Any material or information in the possession or knowledge of the Crown, which is capable of demonstrating ...

Copies of any documentation not already in evidence demonstrating ....This request includes, but is not limited to, items ... on the MG6C schedule.

A full and up-to-date list of keywords used for searches of electronic material, particularly in relation to the exercise of the disclosure exercise for all defendants.

All previously undisclosed records, notes and written statements from interviews with defendants and/or suspects and/or actual or potential witnesses, including, but not limited to, items ... on the MG6C schedule of unused material.

All previously undisclosed reports for computers, electronic devices and mobile telephones seized from defendants and/or suspects.

The fact of, and conclusions from, any ... investigation into the ... background of the Defendant and/or any other defendant/alleged co-conspirator.

Details of any previous convictions and/or complaints against any prosecution witnesses.

It would also assist the Defence to know of any convictions, evidence or information (including intelligence) which establishes a propensity to ... This request would also include any material not already served capable of supporting an allegation that ... was engaged in ... to enable the Defence properly to consider a bad character application in relation to him.

This request includes, but is not limited to, items ... on the MG6C schedule.

Details of any previous convictions and/or complaints against any co-defendants and/or alleged co-conspirator.

Confirmation is sought that the MG6C that has been served is complete.

Any further or revised schedule of unused material (the schedule served to date is dated ... and the final entry is for item ...).

Sensitive Material

i. Has a schedule of sensitive material been prepared?

ii. Has the prosecutor been informed separately of the existence of material deemed to be too sensitive to be included in the schedule?

iii. Has the prosecutor been separately informed of information about (a) any prosecution witness' previous convictions (including spent convictions), (b) disciplinary matters relating to a police officer in this case or (c) previous cases halted/quashed as a result of the conduct of any such officer?

iv. If the answer to (i), (ii) and/or (iii) above is "yes", has the prosecutor decided that they are not under a duty to disclose that material, and/or is an application to be made (or has an application been made) to the court to order the non-disclosure of that material?

Non-relevant Material

When was the last time that any material in the possession of the prosecution, previously deemed to be non-relevant, was reviewed?

Signed .... Dated ....

DEFENCE WITNESS NOTICE

(Criminal Procedure and Investigations Act 1996, section 6C; Criminal Procedure and Investigations Act 1996 (Defence Disclosure Time Limits) Regulations 2011; Criminal Procedure Rules, rule 15.4)

Case details

Name of defendant:

Court:

Case reference number:

Charge(s):

When to use this form

Under section 6C of the Criminal Procedure and Investigations Act 1996, if you are a defendant pleading not guilty you must:

(a) let the court and the prosecutor know **whether you intend to call anyone other than yourself as a witness at your trial;**

(b) do so **not more than -**

14 days (in a magistrates' court case)

28 days (in a Crown Court case)

after initial prosecution disclosure (or notice from the prosecutor that there is no material to disclose);

(c) give as many details of each witness as you can (see the list below);

(d) let the court and the prosecutor know if you later -

(i) decide to call a witness, other than yourself, whom you have not already identified in a defence witness notice,

(ii) decide not to call a witness you have listed in a notice, or

(iii) discover information which you should have included in a notice if you had known it then.

How to use this form

1. Complete the case details box above and give the details required below.

2. Sign and date the completed form.

3. Send a copy of the completed form to:

(a) the court, and

(b) the prosecutor

before the time limit expires.

If you need more time, you **must** apply to the court **before** the time limit expires. You should apply in writing, but no special form is needed.

List of intended defence witness(es)

1. Do you intend to call anyone other than yourself as a witness at your trial ? No ☐ Yes ☐ If yes, give details below. If you use an electronic version of this form, the boxes will expand. If you use a paper version and need more space, you may attach extra sheets.

Name	**Date of birth** (if known)	**Address, or any other contact or identifying details**

2. Have you given a defence witness notice in this case before?

No ☐ **Yes** ☐ If yes, give the date(s).

Signed: ....**[defendant / defendant's solicitor]**

Date: ....

WARNING: Under section 11 of the Criminal Procedure and Investigations Act 1996, **if you (a) do not give a defence witness notice before the time limit expires, or (b) at trial, call a witness whom you have not identified in a witness notice then the court, the prosecutor or another defendant may comment on that, and the court may draw such inferences as it thinks proper in deciding whether you are guilty.**

CHAPTER FIVE

DISCLOSURE REQUESTS

This chapter considers the process for making disclosure requests.

Disclosure requests can be made by the defence at any stage of the proceedings, irrespective of whether initial disclosure has been made and regardless of whether a defence statement has been served. There is nothing to prevent a defence solicitor writing to the prosecution to request disclosure of material or the defence advocate from asking for an item of disclosure from prosecution counsel at court.

The defence's hand is, however, strengthened when it comes to making disclosure requests by the service of a defence statement. Not only does a defence statement help to demonstrate why the material or items sought pass the disclosure test but it also triggers the defence's ability to seek an order from the court compelling the prosecution to provide disclosure.

It is good practice to use a proforma for submitting all disclosure requests. This formalises the request process. An example of a disclosure request pro-forma for use during a trial is enclosed at the end of this chapter.

Defence practitioners should sequentially number and date each disclosure request. This results in easier marshalling of disclosed material, making further requests or responses and drafting written applications to the prosecution and court.

Section 8 applications

Section 8 of the CPIA states:

> *"8.— Application by accused for disclosure.*

(1) This section applies where the accused has given a defence statement … and the prosecutor has complied with section 7A(5) or has purported to comply with it or has failed to comply with it.

(2) If the accused has at any time reasonable cause to believe that there is prosecution material which is required by section 7A to be disclosed to him and has not been, he may apply to the court for an order requiring the prosecutor to disclose it to him.

(3) For the purposes of this section prosecution material is material—

(a) which is in the prosecutor's possession and came into his possession in connection with the case for the prosecution against the accused.

(b) which, in pursuance of a code operative under Part II, he has inspected in connection with the case for the prosecution against the accused, or

(c) which falls within subsection (4).

(4) Material falls within this subsection if in pursuance of a code operative under Part II the prosecutor must, if he asks for the material, be given a copy of it or be allowed to inspect it in connection with the case for the prosecution against the accused.

(5) Material must not be disclosed under this section to the extent that the court, on an application by the prosecutor, concludes it is not in the public interest to disclose it and orders accordingly.

(6) Material must not be disclosed under this section to the extent that it is material the disclosure of which is prohibited by section 56 of the Investigatory Powers Act 2016."

Section 56 of the *Investigatory Powers Act* 2016 relates to intercepted communications. Section 56(1) provides that,

> *"(1) No evidence may be adduced, question asked, assertion or disclosure made or other thing done in, for the purposes of or in connection with any legal proceedings or Inquiries Act proceedings which (in any manner)-*
>
> *(a) discloses, in circumstances from which its origin in interception-related conduct may be inferred-*
>
> *(i) any content of an intercepted communication, or*
>
> *(ii) any secondary data obtained from a communication, or*
>
> *(b) tends to suggest that any interception-related conduct has or may have occurred or may be going to occur..."*

Rule 15.5 of the Criminal Procedure Rules

Reference should also be made to the Criminal Procedure Rules when making a section 8 application. CrimPR 15.5 states,

> ***"Defendant's application for prosecution disclosure***
>
> ***15.5.****—(1) This rule applies where the defendant—*
>
> *(a) has served a defence statement given under the Criminal Procedure and Investigations Act 1996; and*
>
> *(b) wants the court to require the prosecutor to disclose material.*
>
> *(2) The defendant must serve an application on—*
>
> *(a) the court officer; and*
>
> *(b) the prosecutor.*
>
> *(3) The application must—*

(a) describe the material that the defendant wants the prosecutor to disclose;

(b) explain why the defendant thinks there is reasonable cause to believe that—

(i) the prosecutor has that material, and

(ii) it is material that the Criminal Procedure and Investigations Act 1996 requires the prosecutor to disclose; and

(c) ask for a hearing, if the defendant wants one, and explain why it is needed.

(4) The court may determine an application under this rule—

(a) at a hearing, in public or in private; or

(b) without a hearing.

(5) The court must not require the prosecutor to disclose material unless the prosecutor—

(a) is present; or

(b) has had at least 10 business days in which to make representations."

Section 8 applications usually follow after there have been written requests for material that have either been refused by the prosecution and/or the prosecution has not engaged with the defence in relation to their requests. It is, therefore, important to bear in mind from both a prosecution and defence perspective, that this correspondence will usually be considered by the trial judge when considering a section 8 application. Practitioners should note that sequentially numbering and dating previous written disclosure requests assists the court's efficiency and understanding in adjudicating upon section 8 applications.

In terms of timing of service of section 8 applications in the Crown Court, this is usually set as the Stage 4 date. However, if the material requested is required to prepare the defence at an early stage, there is no prohibition on the timing of section 8 applications, post written refusal of disclosure by the Crown. Please see PTPH form at the end of **Chapter Three.**

Focusing the disclosure requests

Sometimes the temptation is to make what are sometimes referred to as "shopping lists", i.e. long lists of disclosure requests which are unjustified and not relevant to an issue in the case. Making targeted and relevant requests, however, is much more likely to lead to a section 8 application being granted and material helpful to the defence being disclosed. In addition, making a series of targeted, sequential applications may expose, and repeatedly expose, any disclosure inadequacies before the court.

As considered in **Chapter Four**, it may also be appropriate to provide a supplementary defence statement, focusing on a particular issue, in order to strengthen a section 8 application.

Inadequate use of section 8 applications means that many disclosure issues are not resolved in advance of the trial to the disadvantage of both the prosecution and defence. It is worth bearing in mind when defending that just informing the judge that there have been repeated disclosure requests is insufficient. The judge might enquire why the defence did not, then, make a section 8 application at an earlier stage.

It is not uncommon for the written section 8 application itself, particularly a well-reasoned one, to prompt the prosecution to disclose the material requested, thereby obviating the need for a hearing at all.

Prescribed form

There is a prescribed form for section 8 applications, which can be found online at:

https://www.gov.uk/government/publications/defendants-application-for-prosecution-disclosure

A copy of this form is also set out at the end of this chapter.

A copy of the defence statement and copies of correspondence with the prosecution in relation to the disclosure requests the subject of the section 8 application should be enclosed with the application itself.

Again, section 8 applications should always provide an explanation as to **why** the item sought is disclosable, in other words, why the item is said to pass the disclosure test.

Examples of disclosure requests

The following are examples of the types of material that you may wish to consider requesting in an appropriate case:

- A copy of the full custody record, including any medical notes for the defendant's periods in police custody during the investigation.

- Previous convictions, cautions and particulars of all allegations and complaints, including unresolved matters relating to prosecution witnesses.

- Confirmation of whether any police officers involved in the case have any disciplinary matters recorded against them; and confirmation as to whether any previous case(s) have been halted or quashed as a result of the conduct of these officers.

- Pocket Notebooks (PNBs) / Incident Report Books (IRBs) of all police officers attending the scene.

- All search records for each address that was searched as part of the investigation.

- Medical notes and reports for the complainant's injuries.

- Any contact logs with the civilian witnesses in the case.

- Any statements provided by the complainant not yet served, howsoever recorded (e.g. including accounts recorded in IRBs, CRIS Reports, Day Books, contact logs, or Body Worn Video footage etc.)

- All statement notes of first accounts taken from civilian witnesses, howsoever recorded.

- Statements from, or identity of, unused witnesses that may contradict or differ from the statements of prosecution witnesses.

- Lists of persons approached who refused to provide witness statements.

- Mobile phone download reports and available billing data for phones associated with the complainant, the defendant and the co-defendant.

- Call data records, in their full format and including full cell site and cell data, obtained by the police in the course of the investigation.

- A copy of any pre-interview disclosure provided to the defendant prior to the interview.

- Copy of the DVD recording of the defendant's interview with the police.

- Confirmation of the existence of CCTV and a description of any steps taken to secure such material.

- Recordings and transcripts of 999 calls.

- Identification parade videos and notes in respect of any identification parade, including first descriptions.

- Details of any relevant information or material which may be in the hands of third parties and contact information for those third parties.

- Details of any compensation claims, including Criminal Injuries Compensation Authority and insurance claims.

- Copy of all Body Worn Video (BWV) footage of the police officers attending the scene.

- Copies of all photographs taken at the scene.

- Clarification of the disposal of other individuals who were arrested but who do not appear on the indictment.

- Any maps or plans of the scene.

- Any previous complaints of a similar nature made by the complainant, and how they were dealt with; for example, no further action taken.

- Any relevant social media posts and messages made by the complainant and a description of any steps taken to secure such material.

- Instructions provided to the prosecution expert.
- Any draft reports that the prosecution expert has previously produced.
- Correspondence, for example emails, between the police and the expert relevant to the preparation of her report. [See **Chapter Eight** in relation to expert witnesses.]

Material which is likely to meet the test for disclosure

The Attorney General's Guidelines on Disclosure (2022) sets out what essentially amounts to a list of items where there is a presumption of disclosure. This is a rebuttable presumption in the sense that the test for disclosure must still be applied. However, it gives the prosecution a useful steer as to the type of material that should ordinarily be disclosed. It also provides the defence with a useful further basis upon which to request unused material if it is not provided as part of initial disclosure.

Paragraph 86 of the Guidelines states:

> *"86. The following material, which is produced and obtained in the majority of investigations is likely to include information which meets the test for disclosure:*
>
> *a) records which are derived from tapes or recordings of telephone messages (for example 999 calls) containing descriptions of an alleged offence or offender;*
>
> *b) any incident logs relating to the allegation;*
>
> *c) crime reports and crime report forms, or where not already contained within the crime report:*
>
> *- an investigation log;*

- any record or note made by an investigator (including police notebook entries and other handwritten notes) on which they later make a statement or which relates to contact with suspects, victims or witnesses;

- an account of an incident or information relevant to an incident noted by an investigator in manuscript or electronically;

- records of actions carried out by officers (such as house-to-house interviews, CCTV or forensic enquiries) noted by a police officer in manuscript or electronically;

- CCTV footage, or other imagery, of the incident in action;

d) the defendant's custody record or voluntary attendance record;

e) any previous accounts made by a complainant or by any other witnesses;

f) interview records (written records, or audio or video tapes, of interviews with actual or potential witnesses or suspects);

g) any material casting doubt on the reliability of a witness e.g. relevant previous convictions and relevant cautions of any prosecution witnesses and any co-accused."

Body Worn Video (BWV) and CCTV footage

Paragraph 87 of the Guidelines specifically addresses CCTV and police body worn video footage, stating that:

*"87. When providing CCTV footage, or other imagery, of the incident in action as material which is likely to meet the test for disclosure, investigators should include all **relevant** body-worn footage that is not provided as evidence. It may be that the entirety of the footage contains both relevant and irrelevant material. Irrelevant footage should not be provided to prosecutors in the first instance. It may be the footage requires clipping or editing to achieve this. Where multiple body worn*

cameras capture the same content, it may be that only one set of footage needs be provided. The remainder should be listed clearly on the unused material schedule. This decision must be made on a case-by-case basis, as it may be that similar but distinct footage has been captured, in which case multiple sets of footage should be provided."

Often, Body Worn Video (BWV) footage contains the first accounts of witnesses at the scene or the defendant's own response on arrest. Sometimes the prosecution may serve a particular officer's body worn footage as evidence but leave the remaining officers' BWV as unused. As with CCTV evidence, the BWV footage may become part of a compilation video, and so it will be important to ensure that any contextual recordings have also been reviewed.

What is shown before and after an incident may be critical and will often, at the very least, provide important context to the evidence. In addition, there may be different camera angles that reveal something not seen in the main footage.

The types of questions that should be asked in relation to disclosure of BWV and CCTV footage include the following:

- What clips have been isolated or bookmarked for viewing?
- To what extent has the disclosure officer viewed the footage?
- Has the content of the footage been clearly set out in the MG6C?
- What is the extent of the footage that has been seized?
- What CCTV was requested and when?
- Was there any CCTV that was lost as a result of not having been requested sooner?

- Is the unused CCTV footage in a viewable format?
- Is the original CCTV footage available to be viewed, on the basis that the quality of that footage is likely to be better than a copy or series of copies?
- Is the time on the footage accurate and, if not, how fast or slow is it?
- Is there a clear description of the location of the CCTV camera at a particular time?
- Did the BWV and CCTV record audio as well?
- Are there any breaks in the footage? This may occur in relation to CCTV cameras that are triggered by the activation of motion sensors.

Notes of contact with prosecution witnesses

One particular category of material that is sometimes not scheduled as it should be is contact between witnesses and the prosecution. This can take the form of contact logs recording any meetings or communications between the prosecution and a witness, draft witness statements that are corrected, email correspondence between an investigating officer and a witness or even new information that is provided by a witness when they attend court for the trial.

In addition, the 'Speaking to Witnesses at Court CPS Guidance', published in February 2018, specifically states the following at page 6:

> *"The record of any meetings between the prosecutor and a witness should be sent to the disclosure officer for scheduling on the MG6 series. When the witness has been spoken to at court on the day of trial, the prosecutor will need to decide whether anything said meets the test for*

disclosure and if it does, to disclose this immediately to the defence, updating the disclosure officer where appropriate."

Custody records and police interviews

In addition to being listed as an example of an item likely to meet the test for disclosure in paragraph 86(d) of the Attorney General's Guidelines on Disclosure (2022), a defendant is also entitled to a copy of his custody record pursuant to paragraph 2.4A of Code C of the *Police and Criminal Evidence Act* 1984 ('PACE').

A defendant is also entitled to a copy of, or access to, a recording of his police interviews, pursuant to paragraphs 4.19 and 7.13 of Code E of PACE.

The custody record and interview recordings should, therefore, be provided to the defence, in the first instance, by the police.

DNA or fingerprints at a crime scene that do not match the defendant

It is important to bear in mind that negative results of forensic tests should also be recorded and, where appropriate, disclosed to the defence. This would include not only a forensic result that identified someone other than the defendant, but also if there was, for example, insufficient DNA material to make any identification at all.

The defence should ensure that, where it is unclear, requests are made to the prosecution to set out the results of any forensic tests that were negative or proved inconclusive.

Defence bad character applications

The defence may wish to make a bad character application in relation to a prosecution witness or co-defendant. In order to do so the defence should be supplied with all the material that they need to make an effective application. If full disclosure is not provided, then a section 8 application should be made to secure the evidence required to support the bad character application.

It should be standard practice that shortly before the trial begins, a further check is made in relation to all prosecution witnesses and defendants to ensure that the antecedents are up-to-date. This check should also include any findings of misconduct against investigating police officers.

It is also a worthwhile precaution for the defence to ask the prosecution at trial to confirm that their PNC checks on prosecution witnesses and co-defendants are up-to-date, particularly in relation to individuals who are already the subject of a bad character application by the defence

Disclosure requests during the trial

During a trial, there may be a number of disclosure requests and responses. In light of the volume and complexity of disclosure now, it is good practice and in the interests of both the prosecution and defence that the requests and responses be provided in dated written requests. Enclosed at the end of this chapter is an example of a pro-forma that can be used for making and responding to disclosure requests during the trial. These should be collated in order to provide a comprehensive record of the disclosure requests and responses.

Responding to disclosure requests

Defence requests should be responded to promptly, in writing, on a point-by-point basis. Where appropriate, the defence should be invited to clarify why a particular request is relevant by reference to the defence statement. It should be remembered that the correspondence in relation to disclosure requests may be considered by the trial judge when deciding a section 8 application. Requests that are ignored, responded to late or not properly considered will only serve to demonstrate to the trial judge that the disclosure exercise is not being conducted as it should be. However, it is also inappropriate to provide disclosure to every single defence request, without proper consideration as to whether the material passes the disclosure test.

Conclusion

Early, targeted disclosure requests, even before a defence statement is served, can help to focus the disclosure exercise. Provided the defence have served a defence statement, they can seek an order from the court pursuant to section 8 of the CPIA that the prosecution do disclose the material requested. The following checklist may assist when making and responding to disclosure requests.

DISCLOSURE REQUESTS CHECKLIST

- o Has a defence statement been served?

- o When is the stage 4 date, or is there another date when section 8 applications have been ordered to be served by?

- o Have the prosecution been asked to disclose a particular item in correspondence?

- o Has a section 8 application been served on the prosecution?

- o Has the defence statement and relevant correspondence been enclosed with the section 8 application?

- o Have the defence articulated, with reference to the defence statement, why the items requested are disclosable? In other words, have the defence presented a list of **reasoned** requests?

- o Have the prosecution confirmed in writing that they refuse to disclose any items requested and, if so, have they explained why?

- o Have previous disclosure requests, which have been refused, been reviewed in light of any further information coming to light or any further representations by the defence?

- o Is it necessary to list the case in order to make a section 8 application to the court? If so, the sooner the case is listed the better.

Section 8 application form

(1) DEFENDANT'S APPLICATION FOR PROSECUTION DISCLOSURE

(1) (Criminal Procedure and Investigations Act 1996, section 8; (2) Criminal Procedure Rules, rule 22.5)

(2) Case details

Name of defendant:

Court:

Case reference number:

Charge(s):

Note: **You must give a defence statement, and allow the prosecutor time to respond, before you can make an application for prosecution disclosure.**

How to use this form

1. Complete the Case details box above and answer the questions set out in the boxes below. If you use an electronic version of this form, the boxes will expand. If you use a paper version and need more space, you may attach extra sheets.

2. Attach to this form:

(a) a copy of your defence statement, and

(b) copies of any correspondence with the prosecutor about disclosure.

3. Sign and date the completed form.
4. Send a copy of the completed form and everything attached to:

(a) the court, and

(b) the prosecutor.

1) What material do you want the prosecutor to disclose ?

2) Why do you think the prosecutor has that material ?

3) Why might that material:

(a) undermine the prosecutor's case against you, or

(b) assist your case ?

4) Do you want the court to arrange a hearing of this application ?
YES / NO

If YES, explain why you think a hearing is needed. (If you do not ask for a hearing, the court may arrange one anyway.)

(1) **Signed:** .... **defendant /**
defendant's solicitor

Date: ....

Trial disclosure request form pro-forma

REQUEST FOR DISCLOSURE OF INFORMATION OR VIEWING OF EXHIBITS / COPY ITEMS FROM UNUSED SCHEDULE

Disclosure request reference:	Request received by:
Defence counsel / solicitor requesting:	Date / Time of Defence Request:
Representing:	Date / Time of Prosecution Response:

<u>DEFENCE</u>: Information requested / disclosure item number (please specify whether disclosure or inspection is sought):
<u>DEFENCE:</u> The requested information / item might reasonably be considered capable of undermining the case for the prosecution against the defendant, or of assisting the case for the defendant, because:
<u>PROSECUTOR'S DECISION:</u> ☐ Disclose (copy) ☐ Disclosure (inspect) ☐ Clearly not disclosable ☐ Not disclosable Name: ……………………….. Signature: ………………………….. Date and time: …………………………..

CHAPTER SIX

DISCLOSURE IN THE MAGISTRATES' COURT

In this chapter we examine the disclosure procedure in the magistrates' court, setting out some common practical problems and solutions.

Attorney General's Guidelines on Disclosure (2022)

Paragraph 96 of the Attorney General's Guidelines on Disclosure (2022) states:

> *"96. In cases heard in the magistrates' court and the youth court, prosecutors should always consider whether or not a disclosure management document (DMD) would be beneficial. DMDs are most likely to be beneficial in cases with the following features:*
>
> *a. Substantial or complex third party material;*
>
> *b. Digital material in which parameters of search, examination or analysis have been set;*
>
> *c. Cases involving international enquiries;*
>
> *d. Cases where there are linked operations;*
>
> *e. Non-recent offending;*
>
> *f. Cases involving material held or sought by the investigation that is susceptible to a claim of legal professional privilege."*

As we set out in **Chapter Three** when considering the timing of initial disclosure, paragraphs 102-104 of the Attorney General's Guidelines on Disclosure (2022) state:

> ***"Cases expected to be tried in the magistrates' court***
>
> *102. Where a case is charged on the Full Code Test and a not guilty plea is anticipated, initial disclosure should be served in advance of the first hearing.*
>
> *103. Where a guilty plea was originally anticipated but a not guilty plea is entered then initial disclosure should be served as soon as possible after a not guilty plea is entered.*
>
> *104. Where a case is charged on the Threshold Test, initial disclosure should be served as soon as possible after the Full Code Test is applied and in accordance with any order made by the court."*

Paragraph 112 of the Attorney General's Guidelines on Disclosure (2022) states:

> ***"Magistrates' court***
>
> *112. Following a not guilty plea being entered in the magistrates' court, the defence must ensure that the trial issues are clearly identified both in court and on the preparation for effective trial form. Prosecutors should ensure that any issues of dispute that are raised are noted on file. The preparation for effective trial form should be carefully reviewed, alongside the DMD (where this exists). Consideration of any issues raised in court or on the form will assist in deciding whether any further material undermines the prosecution case or assist the accused."*

Paragraph 124 of the Attorney General's Guidelines on Disclosure (2022) states:

> *"124. There is no requirement for a defence statement to be served in the magistrates' court but it should be noted that if one is not provided the court does not have a power to hear an application for further prosecution disclosure under section 8 of the CPIA 1996."*

CPIA Code of Practice (2020)

Paragraph 6.3 of the CPIA Code of Practice (2020) states:

> *"6.3 The disclosure officer must ensure that the appropriate schedule of unused material is prepared in the following circumstances…*
>
> - *the accused is charged with an either-way offence that is likely to remain in the magistrates' court, and it is considered that they are likely to plead not guilty;*
> - *the accused is charged with a summary offence and it is considered that they are likely to plead not guilty."*

Paragraph 6.4 of the CPIA Code of Practice (2020) states:

> *"6.4 Where, however, the accused is charged with a summary offence or an either-way offence, and it is considered that they are likely to plead guilty (e.g. because they have admitted the offence), a schedule is not required unless a not guilty plea is subsequently entered or indicated."*

Paragraph 10.4 of the CPIA Code of Practice (2020) states:

> *"10.4 Other than early disclosure under Common Law, in the magistrates' court the schedule (and any relevant unused material to be disclosed under it) must be disclosed to the accused either:*
>
> - *at the hearing where a not guilty plea is entered, or*
> - *as soon as possible following a formal indication from the accused or representative that a not guilty plea will be entered at the hearing."*

CPS Disclosure Manual (Refreshed: 2022)

It is important to note the wording of Chapter 6 of the CPS Disclosure Manual (Refreshed: 2022):

> *"There is no longer a discrete approach to summary disclosure. The Code and the AG's Guidelines no longer distinguish between Streamlined Disclosure Certificates and MG6C. The generic term "schedules" is used instead. Both SDCs and the MG6 series are expected to continue to be used, as agreed locally. The template for Streamlined Disclosure Certificates may still be used for anticipated not guilty plea cases which are reasonably expected to be suitable for summary trial. These should be provided to the prosecutor in accordance with DG6."*

Disclosure at common law / '*ex parte Lee* obligations'

The prosecution must provide disclosure at an early stage. Sometimes, the common law disclosure obligations that apply before the time when the prosecution makes initial disclosure pursuant to section 3 of the CPIA, are referred to as '*ex parte* Lee obligations'.

In *R v DPP, ex parte Lee* [1999] 1 W.L.R. 1950, at 1962-1963, the Court of Appeal set out the following propositions:

> *"(1) The Act of 1996 considerably reduced the ability of the defence to take an active part in committal proceedings, so the need for disclosure prior to committal was also reduced.*
>
> *(2) Part I of the Act introduced a completely new regime in relation to disclosure. It replaces most if not all of the provisions of the common law from the moment of committal with a two-stage process set out in sections 3 and 7. The second stage only occurs in response to a defence statement.*

(3) The disclosure required by the Act of 1996 is, and is intended to be, less extensive than would have been required prior to the Act at common law.

(4) Although some disclosure may be required prior to committal (and thus prior to the period to which the Act of 1996 applies) it would undermine the statutory provisions if the pre-committal discovery were to exceed the discovery obtainable after committal pursuant to the statute.

(5) The Act of 1996 does not specifically address the period between arrest and committal, and whereas in most cases prosecution disclosure can wait until after committal without jeopardising the defendant's right to a fair trial, the prosecutor must always be alive to the need to make advance disclosure of material of which he is aware (either from his own consideration of the papers or because his attention has been drawn to it by the defence) and which he, as a responsible prosecutor, recognises should be disclosed at an earlier stage. Examples canvassed before us were (a) previous convictions of a complainant or deceased if that information could reasonably be expected to assist the defence when applying for bail; (b) material which might enable a defendant to make a pre-committal application to stay the proceedings as an abuse of process; (c) material which might enable a defendant to submit that he should only be committed for trial on a lesser charge, or perhaps that he should not be committed for trial at all; (d) material which will enable the defendant and his legal advisers to make preparations for trial which may be significantly less effective if disclosure is delayed (e.g. names of eye-witnesses who the prosecution do not intend to use).

(6) Clearly any disclosure by the prosecution prior to committal cannot normally exceed the primary disclosure which after committal would be required by section 3 of the Act of 1996, i.e. disclosure of material which in the prosecutor's opinion might undermine the case for the prosecution. However, to the extent that a defendant or his solicitor chooses to reveal what he would normally only disclose in his defence statement, the prosecutor may in advance, if justice requires, give the

> *secondary disclosure which such a revelation would trigger, so whereas no difficulty would arise in relation to disclosing material of the type referred to in sub-paragraphs 5(a)–(c) above, and I accept that such material should be disclosed, the disclosure of material of the type referred to in sub-paragraph 5(d) would depend very much on what the defendant chose to reveal about his case.*
>
> *(7) No doubt additions can be made to the list of material which in a particular case ought to be disclosed at an early stage, but what is not required of the prosecutor in any case is to give what might be described as full blown common law discovery at the pre-committal stage. Although the Act of 1996 has not abolished pre-committal discovery the provisions of the Act taken as whole are such as to require that the common law obligations in relation to the pre-committal period be radically recast in the way that I have indicated.*
>
> *(8) Within the framework which I have attempted to outline I would accept [the] submission that, even before committal, a responsible prosecutor should be asking himself what if any immediate disclosure justice and fairness requires him to make in the particular circumstances of the case. Very often the answer will be none, and rarely if at all should the prosecutor's answer to that continuing piece of self-examination be the subject matter of dispute in this court. If the matter does have to be ventilated it should, save in a very exceptional case, be before the trial judge."*

There are no longer committal proceedings and, as we have discussed in **Chapter Three**, primary and secondary disclosure have now been replaced with initial and continuing disclosure. However, the principles set out in *ex parte Lee* are still relevant to the period before duties under the CPIA arise. As was stated at paragraph 41 of the Magistrates' Court Disclosure Review (May 2014),

> *"R v DPP, ex parte Lee makes it clear that the CPIA did not abolish common law duties regarding the disclosure of material prior to*

> *committal proceedings. The prosecutor must consider the possible need to make disclosure at an early stage."*

Paragraphs 43-44 of the Review went on to state:

> *"43. We therefore underline the need for the prosecution to have in mind their common law/ex parte Lee duties, particularly in cases where there is a lengthy period between arrest and charge. Such duties should be considered from the point of arrest, particularly in cases where there may be a need to disclose unused witness details/statements, which may be critical to the defence.*
>
> *44. We acknowledge that this is not likely to arise frequently in cases tried summarily; however it must still be considered. We envisage that any such material should be disclosed to the defence in advance of the first hearing."*

It could be said, therefore, that there are potentially five phases of disclosure in any given case:

- Common law / *ex parte Lee* disclosure
- Initial disclosure
- Continuing disclosure
- Common law disclosure relevant to sentence (post-conviction)
- Common law disclosure relevant to the safety of the conviction (post-conviction and sentence)

We considered the latter four phases in **Chapter Three**.

Streamlined Summary Disclosure

The CPS Guidance on Streamlined Summary Disclosure (Updated: 20 December 2018) provides that:

> *"…in every case, irrespective of the anticipated plea, if there is material known to the officer in the case/disclosure officer (e.g. a key prosecution witness has relevant previous convictions, or a witness has withdrawn his or her statement) and this material may assist the defence with the early preparation of their case or at a bail hearing, a note must be made on the MG5/DCF…, a copy of which is given to the defence, and the material disclosed to the prosecutor who will disclose it to the defence if he/she thinks it meets the test."*

The Guidance goes on to state that,

> *"Any case file which contains an offence which is indictable only, or is likely not to be suitable for summary trial, must have disclosure prepared in the usual way, by completing the MG6 forms. This includes youth cases that are likely to be considered to be 'grave crimes' and therefore sent to the Crown Court."*

We looked at these MG6 forms in **Chapter Two**, i.e. the MG6C, MG6D and MG6E.

The CPS Guidance on Streamlined Summary Disclosure goes on to state,

> *"The streamlined certificate (SDC) for anticipated not guilty plea (NGAP) cases must be completed for all summary only cases, and all those which are either way but assessed to be clearly suitable for summary trial.*
>
> *There is no requirement to complete a certificate for anticipated guilty plea (GAP) cases. For NGAP and cases where a NG plea is entered to a GAP case, there are two versions of the streamlined certificate. The first should be used when the police officer believes that there is nothing which is disclosable; the second should be used where a police officer believes some material needs to be disclosed.*
>
> *Investigators and prosecutors are reminded of the common law duty under* [1999] 2 All ER 737 DPP ex parte Lee. *The declaration on*

the MG5/Digital Case File (DCF) must be endorsed in the normal way if there is nothing to disclose. If there is something to disclose, its existence should be endorsed on the MG5/DCF. The common law duty applies to both GAP and NGAP cases, so if the MG5 is sent to the CPS before the DCF (for example in custody cases), the certificate must be endorsed or the procedure … below followed.

To summarise:

- *in every case, irrespective of the anticipated plea,*
- *if there is material known to the officer in the case/disclosure officer (e.g. a key prosecution witness has relevant previous convictions, or a witness has withdrawn his or her statement)*
- *and this material may assist the defence with the early preparation of their case or at a bail hearing,*
- *a note must be made on the MG5/DCF…, a copy of which is given to the defence, and*
- *the material disclosed to the prosecutor who will disclose it to the defence if he/she thinks it meets the test."*

Anticipated Guilty Plea (GAP) cases

The CPS Guidance on Streamlined Summary Disclosure then addresses Anticipated Guilty Plea (GAP) cases

"In a case where an officer anticipates after applying the Director's Guidance that a guilty plea will be entered, he/she needs to either:

a) Certify on the MG5/DCF that there is no material that falls to be disclosed under the common law duty to disclose material which might assist the defence with the early preparation of their case or a bail hearing or

b) note such material on the MG5/DCF to bring it to the attention of the prosecutor.

If, exceptionally, that material is sensitive, the sensitive material schedule MG6D (or similar), together with an MG6E, should be used to communicate that to the prosecutor. This/they should be attached to the file in the usual way.

Where material has been identified by an officer, the prosecutor must consider whether it falls to be disclosed. If it does, it must be disclosed accordingly with the IDPC or at court, before the case is heard.

If at the first hearing, the defendant enters a guilty plea, then, subject to any common law duty described above, disclosure of unused material is not triggered. There is no requirement for any further disclosure to the defence. If, at the first hearing in a GAP court, the defendant enters a not guilty plea, the prosecutor should ask the police to submit any additional material required for an NGAP file as soon as possible. The 'Unused Material Certificate for Anticipated NGPs' must be completed at this stage regardless of whether any other material is required. 'Routine revelation' (which means copies of the crime report and the log of messages should be routinely copied to the prosecutor in every case in which a full file is provided. These documents are known in different police forces by different names, for example the incident record report or CAD for the log of messages) should also be provided at this stage; guidance on what should be provided can be found in the Disclosure Manual (Revelation of the material to the prosecutor).

The guidance in section Anticipated Not Guilty Plea (NGAP) Requirements below should then be followed"

Anticipated Not Guilty Plea (NGAP) cases

The CPS Guidance on Streamlined Summary Disclosure then addresses Anticipated Not Guilty Plea (NGAP) cases:

"When preparing the first hearing file, the officer in the case (Or, if one has been appointed, the disclosure officer) must complete the 'Unused Material Certificate for Anticipated NGAPs' … Where the officer believes there is nothing to disclose, he/she should complete the first NGAP version; where he/she thinks there may be something to disclose he/she should complete the second NGAP version. 'Routine revelation' should be provided at the same time.

If there is no material which is sensitive or which might fall to be disclosed as undermining the prosecution case or assisting the defence, the officer should sign the declaration in the relevant section on the 'nothing to disclose' version. If the prosecutor disagrees with that assessment, he/she should endorse the form accordingly and request any material that needs to be disclosed.

…

When the prosecutor receives the file, he/she should consider the completed 'Unused Material Certificate for Anticipated NGAPs' and make an assessment as to whether the material identified falls to be disclosed. The prosecutor should endorse this decision on the form. If the prosecutor disagrees with the officer that something needs to be disclosed, the assessment should be edited to that effect. If in a case where there is nothing to disclose, the prosecutor cannot be satisfied on the descriptions, he/she should request further information and/or inspect the document in question.

A copy of the form and any disclosable material (redacted if necessary) should be available to give to the defence, either at the first hearing in the magistrates' court, or with the IDPC if the prosecutor is aware of representation in advance (Whilst the trigger to disclose is a NGAP, the law does not prevent a prosecutor dealing with disclosure at an earlier stage if necessary and appropriate).

For cases involved streamlined forensic reporting, all notes and material available need to be considered for the purposes of common law and streamlined disclosure prior to the first hearing. Once the forensic service provider has completed his/her report, the officer will need to consider the content, and provide an additional SDC.

If the defence produce a defence statement, the prosecutor may request the police to produce an MG6E."

Defence statements in the magistrates' court

The key difference between summary only cases, or either way offences which remain in the magistrates' court, and Crown Court cases, is that, pursuant to section 6 of the CPIA, the defence are not required to serve a defence statement in magistrates' court proceedings.

Otherwise, the disclosure principles are the same as in the Crown Court. As was set out in paragraph 36 of the Magistrates' Court Disclosure Review (May 2014),

> *"It is important to reiterate that the same disclosure test applies to all criminal prosecutions, whether they take place in a magistrates' or Crown Court. The defence are entitled to expect that the prosecution will have complied with its CPIA obligations regardless of venue. If the prosecution has failed to discharge its obligations by the date of trial, the prosecutor will not be entitled to continue, if s/he is satisfied that a fair trial cannot take place."*

The fact that service of a defence statement is voluntary, does not mean that one should not be served. There are obvious advantages to the defence in serving a defence statement:

- Service of a detailed defence statement has the practical effect of prompting the prosecution to further review its material and to disclose to the defence any material which, in light of the contents of the defence statement, might reasonably be considered capable of assisting the defence or of undermining the prosecution.

- A section 8 application cannot be made unless a defence statement has been served.

- The service of a defence statement sends a clear signal to the court that the defence are aware of and have engaged in the disclosure process, making the court more likely to be sympathetic towards other aspects of the defence case.

Notification of intention to call defence witnesses

It should be noted that although service of a defence statement is not mandatory in the magistrates' court, service of a notification to call defence witnesses **is** obligatory, just as it is in the Crown Court. See section 6C CPIA, set out in **Chapter Four**.

Expected defence witnesses should be set out in section 11 of the Preparation for effective trial form.

Alibi witnesses

If a defence statement is served in advance of a summary trial, it must comply with the requirements of section 6A(2) of the CPIA, i.e. it must set out the name, address and date of birth of any witness the accused believes is able to give evidence in support of an alibi, or at least those details that are known to the accused, together with any information the accused has that would assist in identifying or finding any such witness.

As already referred to in Chapter Four, paragraph 34 of the Court of Appeal decision in *Re Joseph Hill & Co, Solicitors* [2014] 1WLR 786 emphasises that the statutory obligation to give the name and address of an alibi is triggered by the defendant's **belief** that the witness is able to give evidence in support of the alibi, not that the alibi witness can or is even willing to give such evidence.

Defence obligations

Annex A to the Magistrates' Court Disclosure Review (May 2014) sets out the defence disclosure obligations in the magistrates' court as follows:

> *"There are limited disclosure obligations on the defence with regard to cases in the Magistrates' Court jurisdiction. The defence role may essentially be considered a reactive one, although there are specific obligations which they must adhere to within the CPIA and Criminal Procedure Rules. Section 6C CPIA requires the defence to supply details of witnesses whom they intend to call within 14 days of the prosecutor completing (or purporting to complete) initial disclosure... These duties apply regardless of whether a defence statement is served.*
>
> *In line with the duty of the parties actively to assist the court in furthering the overriding objective of the Criminal Procedure Rules by active case management, it is best practice for them to identify the issues as soon as possible.*
>
> *Defence statements should therefore be sufficiently detailed and respond to the prosecution case. Provision of a defence statement will enable the prosecutor to make informed decisions as to whether further material falls to be disclosed. If required, the defence should then make focused and proportionate applications to the court for material to be disclosed under section 8 CPIA."*

Rule 1.1 of the Criminal Procedure Rules sets out the overriding objective as follows,

> ***"The overriding objective***
>
> ***1.1.****—(1) The overriding objective of this procedural code is that criminal cases be dealt with justly.*
>
> *(2) Dealing with a criminal case justly includes—*

(a) acquitting the innocent and convicting the guilty;

(b) treating all participants with politeness and respect;

(c) dealing with the prosecution and the defence fairly;

(d) recognising the rights of a defendant, particularly those under Article 6 of the European Convention on Human Rights;

(e) respecting the interests of witnesses, victims and jurors and keeping them informed of the progress of the case;

(f) dealing with the case efficiently and expeditiously;

(g) ensuring that appropriate information is available to the court when bail and sentence are considered; and

(h) dealing with the case in ways that take into account—

(i) the gravity of the offence alleged,

(ii) the complexity of what is in issue,

(iii) the severity of the consequences for the defendant and others affected, and

(iv) the needs of other cases."

Initial Details of the Prosecution Case (IDPC)

The prosecution's duty to provide initial details of the prosecution case (IDPC) in the magistrates' court is set out in Part 8 of the Criminal Procedure Rules:

"Providing initial details of the prosecution case

8.2.—(1) The prosecutor must serve initial details of the prosecution case on the court officer—

(a) as soon as practicable; and

(b) in any event, no later than the beginning of the day of the first hearing.

(2) Where a defendant requests those details, the prosecutor must serve them on the defendant—

(a) as soon as practicable; and

(b) in any event, no later than the beginning of the day of the first hearing.

(3) Where a defendant does not request those details, the prosecutor must make them available to the defendant at, or before, the beginning of the day of the first hearing.

Content of initial details

8.3. Initial details of the prosecution case must include—

(a) where, immediately before the first hearing in the magistrates' court, the defendant was in police custody for the offence charged—

(i) a summary of the circumstances of the offence, and

(ii) the defendant's criminal record, if any;

(b) where paragraph (a) does not apply—

(i) a summary of the circumstances of the offence,

(ii) any account given by the defendant in interview, whether contained in that summary or in another document,

(iii) any written witness statement or exhibit that the prosecutor then has available and considers material to plea, or to the allocation of the case for trial, or to sentence,

(iv) the defendant's criminal record, if any, and

(v) any available statement of the effect of the offence on a victim, a victim's family or others.

Use of initial details

8.4.*—(1) This rule applies where—*

(a) the prosecutor wants to introduce information contained in a document listed in rule 8.3; and

(b) the prosecutor has not—

(i) served that document on the defendant, or

(ii) made that information available to the defendant.

(2) The court must not allow the prosecutor to introduce that information unless the court first allows the defendant sufficient time to consider it."

It is important to bear in mind that the IDPC is not the same as initial disclosure. As was stated in the Magistrates' Court Disclosure Review (2014),

"29. A common complaint we have heard is that the IDPC is often referred to as 'initial disclosure', or 'advance disclosure', neither of which is correct and both only serve to confuse.

> *30. IDPC information should be sufficient to enable pleas to be taken or to inform allocation decisions for either way cases. It is also expected to be sufficient to enable satisfactory, detailed completion of the effective trial preparation form..."*

Disclosure issues in the magistrates' court

Let us now turn to consider some practical disclosure problems that can arise:

- Late service of papers.
- No or late provision of initial disclosure.
- Cases adjourned for disclosure to take place.
- The prosecution drop the case in light of inadequate disclosure.
- The trial proceeds, despite the disclosure exercise having been properly completed.
- Clients may not be met sufficiently in advance to provide details of their defence.
- Advocates are often not instructed until the day before the trial, by which time it often too late to make any meaningful disclosure requests.
- If disclosure is requested, it may not be provided (if at all) until the day of trial.
- If disclosure is provided late, on the day of trial, the defence may not be given adequate time to consider it by the court.

There is scope on the Preparation for effective trial form to set out the disputed issues of fact and law. Whilst this document cannot be said to be a defence statement, the prosecution still have a continuing duty to review disclosure and so providing sufficient detail on this form should prompt them to review the disclosure that they have carried out. Difficulties arise when this form is not properly or comprehensively completed, so that the prosecution are not alerted to the key issues in advance of the trial. A copy of the form can be downloaded at: https://www.justice.gov.uk/courts/procedure-rules/criminal/docs/2014/crimpr-part3-magistrates-courts-trial-preparation-form.pdf

Applications to adjourn in the magistrates' court

The leading authority on the points to take into account when considering an application to adjourn a trial in the magistrates' court is the case of *CPS v Picton* (2006) 170 JP 567. The Divisional Court, having reviewed the authorities, set out the following principles at paragraph 9:

> *"(a) A decision whether to adjourn is a decision within the discretion of the trial court. An appellate court will interfere only if very clear grounds for doing so are shown.*
>
> *(b) Magistrates should pay great attention to the need for expedition in the prosecution of criminal proceedings; delays are scandalous; they bring the law into disrepute; summary justice should be speedy justice; an application for an adjournment should be rigorously scrutinised.*
>
> *(c) Where an adjournment is sought by the prosecution, magistrates must consider both the interest of the defendant in getting the matter dealt with, and the interest of the public that criminal charges should be adjudicated upon, and the guilty convicted as well as the innocent acquitted. With a more serious charge, the public interest that there be a trial will carry greater weight.*

(d) Where an adjournment is sought by the accused, the magistrates must consider whether, if it is not granted, he will be able fully to present his defence and, if he will not be able to do so, the degree to which his ability to do so is compromised.

(e) In considering the competing interests of the parties the magistrates should examine the likely consequences of the proposed adjournment, in particular its likely length, and the need to decide the facts while recollections are fresh.

(f) The reason that the adjournment is required should be examined and, if it arises through the fault of the party asking for the adjournment, that is a factor against granting the adjournment, carrying weight in accordance with the gravity of the fault. If that party was not at fault, that may favour an adjournment. Likewise if the party opposing the adjournment has been at fault, that will favour an adjournment.

(g) The magistrates should take appropriate account of the history of the case, and whether there have been earlier adjournments and at whose request and why.

(h) Lastly, of course the factors to be considered cannot be comprehensively stated but depend upon the particular circumstances of each case, and they will often overlap. The court's duty is to do justice between the parties in the circumstances as they have arisen."

Abuse of process arguments in the magistrates' court

Please refer to **Chapter Twelve** and the case of *Horseferry Road Magistrates Court, ex parte Bennett* [1994] 1 AC 42, at 64, in which the House of Lords gave guidance in relation to the jurisdiction of the magistrates' court in relation to abuse of process applications. Where the submission is on the basis that it would be unfair to try the defendant (as opposed to on the basis that he cannot receive a fair trial) the application should be made to the High Court.

CHAPTER SEVEN

DIGITAL MATERIAL

Digital material creates potentially the greatest challenge to those tasked with reviewing unused material. What is required is an effective strategy to review the material and to clearly communicate the approach that has been taken.

As is stated in paragraph 55 of the Attorney General's Guidelines on Disclosure (2022), *"The exponential increase in the use of technology in society means that many routine investigations are increasingly likely to have to engage with digital material of some form."* This does not just apply in large and complex prosecutions but also to seemingly "routine" cases involving a smartphone with cloud storage and possibly a number of previous sim cards used in the handset.

A good starting point in cases where there is digital unused material, is to ask the following questions:

- Does the Disclosure Management Document set out clearly the prosecution's approach to digital material?

- Is the continuity of the seizure and exhibiting of all the digital devices established?

- Who accessed the data on the digital devices on the first occasion post-seizure? What was the date and time of initial access of the devices? It is crucial to ask these questions of the prosecution, in order to maintain the integrity of the metadata on the seized devices. The devices post-seizure should be accessed initially by a forensic expert whose task it is to copy all the data from the said devices. Any searches by the investigating team, thereafter, must be conducted on the forensic copy obtained, as opposed to the devices directly. Searching directly upon the devices may alter the metadata each time the device and or data is accessed.

- Is there a schedule of all digital devices, including mobile phones, seized by the police?

- Have the defence been given an opportunity to provide their own keywords for searching the material?

- What Boolean searches have been conducted? A Boolean search is used to define the relationship between search terms, for example using AND, OR and NOT. These types of searches can be used to either narrow or broaden a search.

- How is the digital material actually searched once the keywords have been run on a particular digital device?

The following provide key guidance in relation to the disclosure of digital material:

- *R v R* [2016] 1 W.L.R. 1872

- The CPS 'Disclosure – A guide to "reasonable lines of enquiry" and communications evidence (14 July 2018)

- The CPS 'Disclosure – Guidelines on Communications Evidence' (26 January 2018, updated 3 August 2022)

- *Bater-James and Mohammed [2020] EWCA Crim 790*

- Annex A of the Attorney General's Guidelines on Disclosure (2022)

R v R

Gross LJ, in the Court of Appeal decision of *R v R* [2016] 1 W.L.R. 1872, set out the proper approach to disclosure, particularly in the context of cases involving a significant amount of digital material. Key extracts from *R v R* are set out below:

"• ***The prosecution is and must be in the driving seat at the stage of initial disclosure***

33 The CPIA so provides and considerations of practicality demand it. It must be emphasised that, at this stage, the true issues in the case may yet be unclear. It is no accident that the statutory scheme places the responsibility for determining whether material falls to be disclosed under section 3 of the CPIA on the prosecution.

34 In order to lead (or drive) disclosure, it is essential that the prosecution takes a grip on the case and its disclosure requirements from the outset. To fulfil its duty under section 3, the prosecution must adopt a considered and appropriately resourced approach to giving initial disclosure. Such an approach must extend to and include the overall disclosure strategy, selection of software tools, identifying and isolating material that is subject to legal professional privilege ("LPP") and proposing search terms to be applied. The prosecution must explain what it is doing and what it will not be doing at this stage, ideally in the form of a "Disclosure Management Document". This document, as recommended by the Review and the Protocol, is intended to clarify the prosecution's approach to disclosure (for example, which search terms have been used and why) and to identify and narrow the issues in dispute. By explaining what the prosecution is—and is not—doing, early engagement from the defence would be prompted. Plainly such an approach requires early and careful preparation from the prosecution, tailored to the needs of the individual case...

- ***The prosecution must then encourage dialogue and prompt engagement with the defence***

35 As is clear from the Rules, the duty of the defence is then to engage with the prosecution and thus assist the court in fulfilling its duty of furthering the overriding objective. It is plain that compliance with the test for initial disclosure calls for analysis of the likely cases of prosecution and defence. Absent such analysis, it would not be possible to form a view, even at this stage, of which materials would and which would not undermine the case for the prosecution and/or assist the case for the accused.

- ***The law is prescriptive of the result, not the method***

36 This is particularly relevant in respect of a case such as this where the prosecution has recovered vast volumes of electronic material. In our judgment, it has been clear for some time that the prosecution is not required to do the impossible, nor should the duty of giving initial disclosure be rendered incapable of fulfilment through the physical impossibility of reading (and scheduling) each and every item of material seized; common sense must be applied. In such circumstances, the prosecution is entitled to use appropriate sampling and search terms and its record-keeping and scheduling obligations are modified accordingly...

37 The extent of the duty imposed on the prosecution at this stage, while obviously fact specific, must take account that it is initial disclosure with which the prosecution is then concerned. The right course at the stage of initial disclosure is for the prosecution to formulate a disclosure strategy, canvass that strategy with the court and the defence and to utilise technology to make an appropriate search or conduct an appropriate sampling exercise of the material seized. That searches and sampling may subsequently need to be repeated (to comply with the prosecutor's continuing duty of disclosure under section 7A of the CPIA or to respond to reasoned requests from the defence under section 8) is neither here nor there; the need for repeat searches and sampling does not invalidate the approach to initial disclosure involving such techniques. The problem of vast quantities of electronic documents has, in a sense, been created by technology; in turn, appropriate use must be made of technology to address and solve that problem.

38 The prosecution's duties of record keeping and scheduling must likewise reflect the reality that not every one of perhaps many millions of e-mails is to be individually referenced. Thus, the 2013 Guidelines, Annex A, paragraphs A45–A46, reflecting the Code of Practice, qualify the requirement to keep a "record or log" of all digital material seized and subsequently retained as relevant to the investigation in cases "involving very large quantities of data"; in such cases, the obligation is to make a record of the "strategy and the analytical techniques used to search the data". Similarly, the scheduling duty imposed on the disclosure officer separately to list each item of unused material (as contained in the Code) is modified in favour of "block listing"—albeit that it remains the prosecution's duty to list and describe separately "the search terms used and any items of material which might satisfy the disclosure test": 2013 Guidelines, Annex A, paragraph A50.

- ***The process of disclosure should be subject to robust case management by the judge, utilising the full range of case management powers***

39 Though decisions are for the prosecutor, such decisions or prosecution failures are not beyond challenge or somehow immune from the court's case management powers. …

41 In our judgment, the judicial task of active and robust case management is emphatically not confined to the secondary or subsequent stages of disclosure… The court is both entitled and obliged to give orders and directions to address the failing with which it is confronted. Neither is the judge required to watch the case become diverted from its proper course, powerless to stop it doing so until much time and costs have elapsed. The wording of section 3 was not intended to give the prosecution carte blanche to under-perform and, as experience has shown, prosecution failures in this area are of real concern...

44 Thus, in the context of initial disclosure, it is incumbent on the judge to consider the obligations of the Crown at that stage, bearing in mind the difficulties (where such exist) of ascertaining the real issues in advance of a defence statement. Moreover, when exercising case management powers at this early stage, it is critical for the court to have regard to the structure of the CPIA scheme—initial disclosure (section 3), followed by a defence statement (section 5), the facility thereafter for a reasoned application by the defence for further disclosure (section 8) and the prosecutor's continuing duty to disclose (section 7A). It should also be plain that, when making case management orders at the stage of initial disclosure, a judge should take care not to subvert the statutory scheme by confusing or conflating the various stages in the process...

48 ... compliance with the prosecutor's duty under section 3 must mean substantial compliance. Realistically, it cannot be supposed that cases will never proceed beyond the stage of initial disclosure merely because some documents have not yet been disclosed. A search for perfection in this area is likely to be illusory. ... both sections 5 and 6 provide for a defence statement to be given not only when the prosecutor has complied with section 3 but also when he has purported to comply with it. Progress can and should thus be made, even where it is or may be apparent that further prosecution disclosure might be required in the future. It also follows that cases are not doomed to proceed in compartmentalised, consecutive stages; progress can be made in parallel, both completing outstanding initial disclosure and illuminating the true issues in the case pursuant to sections 5, 6, 7A and 8.

• ***Flexibility is critical***

49 Both the review and all other source materials on disclosure emphasise that it is not to be conducted as a "box-ticking" exercise ... In a document heavy case (whether electronic or paper) there can therefore be no objection in principle to the judge, after discussion with the parties, devising a tailored or bespoke approach to disclosure. That must certainly be preferable to dealing with the matter in a mechanistic and unthinking way..."

50 ... The constant aim must be to make progress, if need be in parallel, from initial disclosure to defence statement, addressing requests for further disclosure in accordance with section 8. If this proviso is overlooked, the real danger is that an apparently attractive "shortcut" will turn out to be a dead-end, leaving all concerned bogged down in satellite litigation over initial disclosure...

52 ... While it is right that attention must be paid to the format of the material supplied ..., it is no part of the prosecution's duty under section 3 to improve the material seized."

A series of extracts from R v R is also helpfully set out in a Practice Note: R v R [2015] EWCA Crim 1941; [2016] 1 Cr. App. R. 20, [2016] 1 WLR 1872.

The CPS 'Disclosure – A guide to "reasonable lines of enquiry" and communications evidence (14 July 2018)

The CPS 'Disclosure – A guide to "reasonable lines of enquiry" and communications evidence' offers particular guidance in those cases where the defendant and complainant are known to each other and where the complainant's smartphone may contain relevant material. The guidance document includes the following:

"13. The examination of mobile devices belonging to the complainant is not a requirement as a matter of course in every case. There will be

cases where there is no requirement for the police to take the media devices of a complainant or others at all, and thus no requirement for even a level 1 examination to be undertaken. Examples of this would include sexual offences committed opportunistically against strangers, or historic allegations where there is considered to be no prospect that the complainant's phone will retain any material relevant to the period in which the conduct is said to have occurred and/or the complainant through age or other circumstances did not have access to a phone at that time...

19. What represents a reasonable line of enquiry is an investigative matter for the police and whilst the prosecution will do what they can to assist in identifying potential further enquiries, that ought not to be taken by the police as definitive or exhaustive."

Referring to the above quoted guidance, the Court of Appeal in *R v E* [2018] EWCA 2426 (Crim), at paragraph 23 stated,

"This guidance appears to us accurately to set out the considerations that investigators should have in mind when deciding what enquiries should be made during investigations into allegations of sexual offences. It should be noted that it does not say that mobile phones should be examined as a matter of course in every case: the decision is fact specific in each and every case."

The CPS 'Disclosure – Guidelines on Communications Evidence' (26 January 2018, updated 3 August 2022)

The CPS 'Disclosure – Guidelines on Communications Evidence' (26 January 2018, updated 3 August 2022) is also directed at those cases where the defendant and complainant have been in a personal relationship. The guidance points out that serious consequences flow from a failure to understand and assess communications evidence which, *"includes communications by way of telephone or other electronic device or by social media and is not restricted to communications between the complainant and suspect but may include contact with third parties".* The *guidelines put the importance of communications in such cases, which included sexual offences, in this way:*

> *"…it would be rare indeed for communications evidence not to feature as part of the police investigation."*

Paragraph 4 of the Guidelines provides the following advice:

- *"Consider asking the suspect or / and complainant whether there might be communication material which may have a bearing on the case.*

- *It is necessary carefully to consider the facts of a particular case, the issues raised and any potential defence in order to decide what amounts to a reasonable line of enquiry.*

- *Prosecutors should provide assistance to investigators when making such a decision and, ideally, agree with them what amounts to a reasonable line of enquiry.*

- *In reaching such a decision, prosecutors are reminded that the whole of a relevant download falls to be considered i.e. all forms of message communication [even if deleted] and photographs / videos if stored. Equally the investigation should not be limited to messages between the complainant and the suspect only as communications between either of them and others may have an impact on the case, for example, when reference is made by either to the events which are the subject of the allegations.*

- *In some cases it may be necessary for the whole of a download to be examined. The extent of any investigation of digital material should only be confined if it is not considered to be a reasonable line of enquiry."*

The Guidelines underscore the fact that disclosure is an ongoing process and that prosecutors must be able to assess the potential impact of communications material before a charging decision is made. Equally, if that material does not become evidence in the case, the telephone or other device and any download deriving from it must be listed on the MG6C schedule as separate items together with a proper description of it.

Bater-James and Mohammed

In *Bater-James and Mohammed* [2020] EWCA Crim 790, the Court of Appeal considered four issues of principle:

(i) Identifying the circumstances when it is necessary for investigators to seek details of a witness's digital communications.

(ii) When it is necessary, how should the review of the witness's electronic communications be conducted?

(iii) What reassurance should be provided to the complainant as to the ambit of the review and the circumstances of any disclosure of material that is relevant to the case?

(iv) What are the consequences of the complainant refuses to permit access to a potentially relevant device of deletes the relevant material?

(i) Identifying the circumstances when it is necessary for investigators to seek details of a witness's digital communications.

In paragraph 77, the Court of Appeal stressed that, *"regardless of the medium in which the information is held, a 'reasonable line of enquiry' will depend on the facts of, and the issues in, the individual case, including any potential defence. There is no presumption that a complainant's mobile telephone or other devices should be inspected, retained or downloaded, any more than there is a presumption that investigators will attempt to look through material held in hard copy. There must be a properly identifiable foundation for the inquiry, not mere conjecture or speculation."*

(ii) When it is necessary, how should the review of the witness's electronic communications be conducted?

The Court of Appeal concluded on this second issue, at paragraph 88, that, *"investigators will need to adopt an incremental approach. First, to consider with care the nature and detail of any review that is required, the particular areas that need to be looked at and whether this can happen without recourse to the complainant's mobile telephone or other device. Second, and only if it is necessary to look at the complainant's digital device or devices, a critical question is whether it is sufficient simply to view limited areas (e.g. an identified string of messages/emails or particular postings on social media). In some cases, this will be achieved by simply looking at the relevant material and taking screenshots or making some other record, without taking possession of, or copying, the device. Third, if a more extensive enquiry is necessary, the contents of the device should be downloaded with the minimum inconvenience to the complainant and, if possible, it should be returned without any unnecessary delay. If the material is voluminous, consideration should be given to appropriately focussed enquiries using search terms, a process in which the defendant should participate. It may be possible to apply data parameters to any search. Finally, appropriate redactions should be made to any disclosed material to avoid revealing irrelevant personal information."*

(iii) What reassurance should be provided to the complainant as to the ambit of the review and the circumstances of any disclosure of material that is relevant to the case?

The Court of Appeal stated at paragraph 92 that, *"the complainant should be told i) that the prosecution will keep him or her informed as to any decisions that are made as to disclosure, including how long the investigators will keep the device; what it is planned to be "extracted" from it by copying; and what thereafter is to be "examined", potentially leading to disclosure; ii) that in any event, any content within the mobile telephone or other device will only be copied or inspected if there is no other appropriate method of discharging the prosecution's disclosure obligations; and iii) material will only be provided to the defence if it meets the strict test for disclosure and it will be served in a suitably redacted form to ensure that personal details or other irrelevant information are not unnecessarily revealed (e.g. photographs, addresses or full telephone numbers)."*

(iv) What are the consequences of the complainant refuses to permit access to a potentially relevant device of deletes the relevant material?

At paragraph 99, the Court of Appeal stated that, *"it is important to look carefully at the reasons for a refusal to permit access and to furnish the witness with an explanation and reassurance as to the procedure that will be followed if the device is made available to the investigator. If it is suggested that the proceedings should be stayed, the court will need to consider the adequacy of the trial process, and whether this will ensure there is fairness to the defendant, particularly by way of cross-examination of the witness, coupled with appropriate judicial directions. The court should not be drawn into guessing at the content and significance of the material that may have become unavailable. Instead, the court must assess the impact of the absence of the particular missing evidence and whether the trial process can sufficiently compensate for its absence. An application can be made for a witness summons for the mobile telephone or other device to be produced. If the witness deletes material, although each case will need to be assessed on its own facts, we stress the potential utility of cross-examination and carefully crafted judicial directions. If the proceedings are not stayed and the trial proceeds, the uncooperative stance by the witness, investigated by appropriate questioning, will be an important factor that the jury will be directed to take into account when deciding, first, whether to accept the evidence of the witness and, second, whether they are sure of the defendant's guilt."*

Annex A of the Attorney General's Guidelines on Disclosure (2022)

Annex A supplements the Attorney General's Guidelines on Disclosure (2022). Paragraph 39 of Annex A states that,

> *"36. "Lines of inquiry, of whatever kind, should be pursued only if they are reasonable in the context of the individual case. It is not the duty of the prosecution to comb through all the material in its possession (e.g.*

every word or byte of computer material) on the lookout for anything which might conceivably or speculatively undermine the case or assist the defence. The duty of the prosecution is to disclose material which might reasonably be considered capable of undermining its case or assisting the case for the accused which they become aware of, or to which their attention is drawn."

Paragraph 44 states that,

> *"44. The digital strategy must be set out in an IMD and subsequently a DMD. This should include the details of any sampling techniques used (including key word searches) and how the material identified as a result was examined."*

Annex A also makes clear that it may be necessary to carry out searches more than once and, in paragraph 45, suggests that it should be considered where:

> *(a) Further evidence or unused material is obtained in the course of the investigation; and/or*
>
> *(b) The defence statement is served on the prosecutor; and/or*
>
> *(c) The defendant makes an application under section 8 of the CPIA 1996 for disclosure; and/or*
>
> *(d) The defendant requests that further sampling or searches be carried out (provided it is a reasonable line of inquiry)."*

Annex A stresses the importance of keeping a proper record of all digital material seized and any searching or analytical processing of that material. The following examples are given at paragraph 48 of details that may be recorded:

> *"(a) A record of all searches carried out, including the date of each search and the person(s) who conducted it.*

> *(b) A record of all search words or terms used on each search. However, where it is impracticable to record each word or term it will usually be sufficient to record each broad category of search.*
>
> *(c) A log of the key judgements made while refining the search strategy in light of what is found, or deciding not to carry out further searches.*
>
> *(d) Where material relating to a "hit" is not examined, the decision not to examine should be explained in the record of examination or in a statement. For instance, a large number of "hits" may be obtained in relation to a particular search word or term, but material relating to the "hits" is not examined because they do not appear to be relevant to the investigation. Any subsequent refinement of the search terms and further hits should also be noted and explained as above."*

However, paragraph 49 of Annex A appears to limit the scope, to some extent, of what the defence can reasonably expect to receive in terms of records of searches:

> *"49. Just as it is not necessary for the investigator or prosecutor to produce records of every search made of hard copy material, it is not necessary to produce records of what may be many hundreds of searches or analyses that have been carried out on digitally stored material simply to demonstrate that these have been done. Instead, the investigator and the prosecutor should ensure that they are able to explain how the disclosure exercise has been approached and to give the accused or suspect's legal representative an opportunity to participate in defining the reasonable searches to be made, as described in the section on sifting/examination."*

Scheduling digital material creates the obvious practical problem in relation to how it is set out in the MG6C. Annex A provides the following practical guidance in relation to this exercise:

> *"51. It will generally be disproportionate in cases involving large quantities of digital data to list each item of material separately. Unless*

it is necessary or otherwise appropriate to separately list each item, the material should be listed in a block or blocks and described by quantity and generic title. Where the material is listed in a block or blocks, the search terms used and any items of material which might satisfy the disclosure test should be listed and described separately. In practical terms this will mean, where appropriate, cross referencing the schedules to the DMD.

52. Where material has been listed in a block and metadata is available for the material within the block, consideration should be given to creating a file of that metadata and listing this separately and linked to the block listing to which it relates.

53. Where continuation sheets of the unused material schedule are used, or additional schedules are sent subsequently, the item numbering must be, where possible, sequential to all other items on earlier schedules. This may include numbering by volume or sub-volume."

In cases where there is a large amount of digital material and keyword searches are conducted by the prosecution, the defence should be invited, usually in correspondence and also the Disclosure Management Document, to themselves supply proposed keywords. These requests should be as focused as possible. The defence should, for example, supply search requests to be run against specific documents, folders or emails, between particular individuals and within a specific timeframe, that they consider pass the disclosure test, explaining why.

It may be appropriate to establish whether a complainant has been asked the extent to which they use digital media and electronic communications. This will provide a useful starting point for identifying reasonable lines of enquiry.

In some circumstances, it may be necessary to seek a full download of a witness or complainant's Facebook or other social media profile on order to review the following:

- Messages or posts sent or received in relation to an important issue in the case.

- Surrounding messages that may provide context to another message the prosecution rely on in evidence.

It is also worth bearing in mind that sometimes it is not just what is said in messages or posts that is important but what is not said that may be equally significant.

The evidence in rape and serious sexual offence prosecutions often comes down to one person's word against the other. The messages exchanged between the defendant and complainant and between them and others have, therefore, significant potential to undermine the prosecution case or to assist the defence case.

Messages exchanged shortly before and after an alleged rape or sexual assault, not just between the complainant and defendant but between the complainant and a close friend may, for example, be highly relevant to the issue of consent.

The defence can seek to ensure that, where appropriate, the prosecution do carry out checks on a complainant's digital media. This can be done by setting out clearly the issues in the defence statement, making section 8 applications where necessary, and scrutinising the prosecution's approach to disclosure.

The prosecution's approach to the review of digital material should be clearly set out in a Disclosure Management Document. This should ensure that any review of digital media is carried out effectively by officers who have received adequate training and who are alive to the issues in the case. It will, for example, be inadequate for the prosecution simply to assert that there is nothing to disclose, without properly setting out how they have approached the task of considering and reviewing digital material. If there are shortcomings, the defence should raise these at the earliest opportunity.

It is also worth considering with care the following question, which appears on the PTPH form at page 3,

> *"Do the defence agree the level of extraction of data and, if not, what level is said to be necessary by reference to the issues in the case?"*

Page 9 of the PTPH form, under Stage 2, also states,

> *"Response to prosecution Disclosure Management Document if served identifying by reference to the issues in the case any disputes as to reasonable lines of enquiry* ***or levels of data extraction****" (emphasis added)*

Please see PTPH form at the end of **Chapter Three**.

Keyword searches

The precise nature of keyword searches is important. A record should, therefore, be kept of any keyword searches, together with any search parameters that were used, and when those searches were conducted and by whom, for future reference.

An advanced search may use filters such as date parameters, file types and location.

The search criteria might include a search for exact words, names or phrases, or seek to find documents excluding particular words or phrases.

Searches may also seek two or more words in proximity, for example a name and a location.

With certain software, the 'fuzziness' of searches may also be adjusted, for example, to take account of typos and spelling errors.

Often there is a degree of trial and error in order to generate a useful set of search criteria to identify relevant and disclosable documents.

Carefully calibrated searches are crucial in cases involving large data pools to ensure that all relevant and disclosable material is captured but that the search results are not too broad so as to create too many false positives.

The client should be asked to provide a set of keywords that may be useful for identifying material that might undermine the prosecution case or assist a particular aspect of the defence case. Such a list should be focused and reviewed by the defence solicitor and defence counsel before being submitted to the prosecution.

Points to consider to help identify the most relevant material might include the following:

- Use of nicknames.
- Use of slang.
- Use of textspeak.
- Use of coded or guarded conversations may require a closer look at the context.
- Limiting the searches to specific time parameters.
- In relation to messages, limiting the search to messages between, from or to specific individuals.
- Limiting the searches to specific folders on a computer.

You may, tactically, not wish to alert the prosecution to particular search terms, or may wish to check the prosecution's analysis of one or more of the electronic devices seized. In those circumstances, requests should be made for either access to, return of, or a forensic copy of, the contents of a given electronic device. If necessary, an expert can be instructed to assist in the search or analysis of the data on a digital device.

In a cut-throat case, or where a particular aspect of a co-defendant's case is challenged, you may also wish to supply keywords to be run against a co-defendant's computer or mobile phone.

Dip sampling

The following is an example of a possible approach to dip sampling electronic material, depending on the number of hits a particular keyword search produces.

c) 100 hits or less – all examined;

d) 101-300 hits – at least 75% examined at random;

e) 301-1,000 hits – at least 50% examined at random;

f) 1,001 – 10,000 hits – at least 5% examined at random;

g) 10,001-100,000 hits – at least 0.5% examined at random;

h) Over 100,000 hits – 500 examined at random.

Whatever the approach, it should be set out for the defence clearly in a Disclosure Management Document. The DMD should not only include a list of the keywords used, but the rationale as to why those words were chosen. In appropriate cases, this document should also set out the list of requested search terms which were not pursued and provide reasons for this decision.

To avoid the process becoming unmanageable, therefore, the review of digital material as part of the disclosure exercise requires a bespoke strategy, tailored to the facts of the particular case. The approach adopted must also be properly communicated to the defence and their active engagement in the process sought.

CHAPTER EIGHT

EXPERT WITNESSES

We consider in this chapter particular points to bear in mind when conducting cases involving expert witnesses.

CPS Disclosure Manual

The following is set out in Chapter 36 of the CPS Disclosure Manual (Refreshed: 21 October 2021):

> *"... The obligations which apply to an expert are to ensure that the prosecution team can comply fully with the requirements of disclosure. These obligations take precedence over any internal codes of practice or other standards set by any professional organisations to which the expert may belong and can be summarised as the key actions of record, retain and reveal.*
>
> *An expert not employed by the police is a third party, and is not bound by the obligations set out in the CPIA as amended. The CPS seeks to impose these obligations as part of the contractual relationship with the expert.*
>
> *The obligations are set out in CPS Guidance for Experts on Disclosure, Unused Material and Case Management (the Guidance for Experts).*
>
> *When an expert is instructed in an investigation, it must be ensured that the expert understands the obligations placed upon them by this status. The expert witness has an overriding duty to assist the court and, in this respect, the expert's duty is to the court, and not to the investigator or prosecutor. This will include obligations relating to disclosure.*

The Guidance for Experts also contains a sample of the index of unused material that an expert will be asked to complete, describing all the unused material in their possession. The expert will not be expected to distinguish between sensitive and non-sensitive material. It is the responsibility of the disclosure officer, in conjunction with the expert, to identify any sensitive material.

The disclosure officer should include the index completed by the expert, on the MG6C/D schedule."

Guidance Booklet for Experts

The 'CPS Guidance Booklet for Experts on Disclosure, Unused Material and Case Management' (updated 30 September 2019) can be downloaded from the CPS website.

Paragraph 4.7 of the Guidance Booklet sets out what is expected of prosecution experts:

"There are three key obligations arising for you, as an expert, as the investigation progresses in order to discharge your obligations. Your understanding of these and your delivery of them is the key to you adequately fulfilling your disclosure obligations. The relevant steps are to ***retain****, to* ***record****, and to* ***reveal****."*

Retain

Paragraph 4.8 of the Booklet states,

"You should retain everything, including physical, written and electronically captured material, until otherwise instructed and the investigator has indicated the appropriate action to take."

Record

Paragraph 4.9.3 of the Booklet states that the expert should keep records of all the work that they have carried out and any findings that they have made in relation to the investigation. It provides the following examples of things that should be recorded as a minimum:

- *the collection and movement of items, including:*
- *the date on which you take or receive material (physical items and information);*
- *and the date of subsequent movement of the material to another party;*
- *from who or where and to whom or where material is moved;*
- *the means by which you receive or pass material from/to another party.*
- *the examination of materials;*
- *your notes, and those of any assistant, should be signed, dated, attributable to the individual and produced contemporaneously, whenever practicable;*
- *the notes should be sufficiently detailed and expressed in such a manner that another expert in your field can follow the nature of the work undertaken;*
- *any assumptions made and the inferences you have drawn from the work;*
- *verbal and other communications;*
- *you should keep your own notes of all meetings you attend;*

- *you should keep your own notes of telephone conversations and it is important that points of agreement, or disagreement and agreed actions are recorded;*

- *you should ensure that a record of all emails and other electronic transmissions (such as images), sent or received, is kept;*

- *you should keep clear notes of any witness accounts or explanations that you have been provided with, or any other information received."*

Reveal

Paragraph 4.10.1 of the Booklet states,

> *"You are required to reveal everything you have recorded to the Prosecution Team. It is a necessary and important part of your disclosure obligations to make the Prosecution Team aware of all the material you have in your possession in relation to the investigation. This will then enable them to make informed decisions as to what material is relevant, and then what material satisfies the disclosure test. Revealing material to the prosecution team does not necessarily mean disclosure to the defence."*

Appendix A of the Booklet sets out a pro-forma of an expert's index of unused material. This includes the following examples of material that might feature in an expert witness's unused schedule:

> *"FORMS detailing receipt and dispatch of items to laboratory; movement of items with[in] and between sites; submission forms detailing nature of offence, work required and details of suspects, victims etc.*
>
> *CASE NOTES made at the time of the examination of the items: provide details of dates of examination. Case file details of packaging*

and integrity of items; records of work performed on the items, who was involved and dates analytical and test results; details of quality checks.

DRAFT REPORTS electronic and or hard copy drafts of reports or statements sent out to police and CPS.

ADMINISTRATIVE DOCUMENTS: time recording sheets; case costings; delivery notes; invoices; records of enquiries with customer relating to costs etc.

MINUTES of conversations with and instructions to other staff; records of conversations and emails with the OIC, police personnel prosecutor and other CPS personnel

RECORDS of material submitted but not examined; of material examined but relating to suspects not included in reports or statements; of work carried out by others, including the results; of procedures and techniques used during the examinations.

RETAINED MATERIALS: material from Items.

SCENE OF CRIME related material: written notes, [voice recorded notes], diagrams, photographs/images taken at the time of the scene attendance.

POST-MORTEM related material: written notes, [voice recorded notes], diagrams, photographs/images taken during the post mortem examination.

WITNESS STATEMENTS from the following people: [name].

ADDITIONAL INFORMATION in the form of: maps, plans, photographs, videos relating to the scene of the offence; details of modus operandi; details of related offences.

DATABASES, material from the following databases have been used: [name of database]."

Expert witness self-certificate

Appendix B of the Guidance Booklet for Experts contains a recommended form of words for the prosecution expert to include in their statement to confirm that they have complied with their disclosure obligations. Described as an expert witness's, *"self-certificate"*, Appendix B includes the following wording:

> *"...I confirm that I have read the CPS Guidance for Experts on Disclosure, Unused Material and Case Management that has been provided with this form, and that I am aware of my responsibilities as an expert witness to reveal to the prosecution team any information that might undermine my evidence or assist the defence.*
>
> *The following information is provided to the prosecution team under Criminal Procedure Rule 19.2(3)(d) to disclose anything of which I am aware, that might reasonably be thought capable of undermining the reliability of my opinion or detracting from my credibility or impartiality...*
>
> *Are you aware of any information that might reasonably be thought capable of undermining the reliability of your opinion or detracting from your credibility or impartiality?*
>
> *Yes/No Please delete as applicable and if the answer is yes please give details below:..."*

Part 19 of the Criminal Procedure Rules

When instructing an expert, it is critical that they are made aware of Part 19 of the Criminal Procedure Rules, which contains procedural obligations in relation to adducing expert evidence.

Rule 19.2: Expert's duties to the court

Rule 19.3: Introduction of expert evidence

Rule 19.4: Content of expert's report

Rule 19.5: Expert to be informed of service of report

Rule 19.6: Pre-hearing discussion of expert evidence

Rule 19.7: Court's power to direct that evidence is to be given by a single joint expert

Rule 19.8: Instructions to a single joint expert

Rule 19.9: Application to withhold information from another party

The Criminal Procedure Rules make specific reference to the obligations placed upon **either** party, i.e. prosecution or defence, who seek to rely on expert evidence.

CrimPR 19.2(3)(d) requires the expert to disclose to the party calling her, anything, *"of which the expert is aware, and of which that party, if aware of it, would be required to give notice under rule 19.3(3)(c)."*

CrimPR 19.3(3) states,

> *"(3) A party who wants to introduce expert evidence otherwise than as admitted fact must-...*
>
> *(c) serve with the report-*
>
> *(i) notice of anything of which the party serving it is aware which might reasonably be thought capable of undermining the reliability of the expert's opinion, or detracting from the credibility or impartiality of the expert..."*

CrimPR 19.3(4) states that,

> *"(4) Unless the parties otherwise agree or the court directs, a party may not-*

(a) introduce expert evidence if that party has not complied with paragraph (3)…"

Criminal Practice Directions 2023

Paragraph 7.1.4 of the Criminal Practice Directions 2023 provides that, *"In order to enable full assessment of the reliability of any expert evidence relied upon, all potentially relevant information must be disclosed, both in relation to the expert and in relation to any corporation or other body with which the expert works, as an employee or in any other capacity"*. The following examples are then given of material that should be disclosed:

"(a) any fee arrangement under which the amount or payment of the expert's fees is in any way dependent on the outcome of the case;

(b) any conflict of interest of any kind, other than a potential conflict disclosed in the expert's report;

(c) adverse judicial comment regarding a particular expert or corporation or other body for whom the expert works whether by a first instance tribunal or on appeal;

(d) any case in which an appeal has been allowed by reason of a deficiency in the expert's evidence;

(e) any adverse finding, disciplinary proceedings or other criticism by a professional, regulatory or registration body or authority, including the Forensic Science Regulator;

(f) any such adverse finding or disciplinary proceedings against, or other such criticism of, others associated with the corporation or other body with which the expert works which calls into question the quality of that corporation's or body's work generally;

(g) conviction of a criminal offence in circumstances that suggest:

(i) a lack of respect for, or understanding of, the interests of the criminal justice system (for example, perjury; acts perverting or tending to pervert the course of public justice),

(ii) dishonesty (for example, theft or fraud), or

(iii) a lack of personal integrity (for example, corruption or a sexual offence);

(h) lack of an accreditation or other commitment to prescribed standards where that might be expected;

(i) a history of failure or poor performance in quality or proficiency assessments;

(j) a history of lax or inadequate scientific methods;

(k) a history of failure to observe recognised standards in the expert's area of expertise;

(l) a history of failure to adhere to the standards expected of an expert witness in the criminal justice system."

Paragraph 7.1.5 of the Criminal Practice Directions 2023 states,

"In a case in which an expert, or a corporation or body with which the expert works, has been criticised without a full investigation, for example by adverse comment in the course of a judgment, it would be reasonable to expect those criticised to supply information about the conduct and conclusions of any independent investigation into the incident, and to explain what steps, if any, have been taken to address the criticism."

Footnote 78 to paragraph 7.1.5 of the Criminal Practice Directions 2023 states,

> *"The rules require disclosure of what the expert, or the party who introduces the expert evidence, is aware. The rules do not require persistent or disproportionate enquiry, and courts will recognise that there may be occasions on which neither the expert nor the party has been made aware of criticism."*

We set out below examples of the sort of questions you should have in mind when considering expert evidence. These questions apply equally whether you are prosecuting or defending. When defending, these questions should be considered to ensure that adequate disclosure has been made by the prosecution. When prosecuting, again these are the sorts of questions you should have in mind, and may be particularly useful if holding a conference with an expert witness in advance of the trial.

EXPERT WITNESS CHECKLIST

- o What is the expertise of the witness? Just because a witness has given evidence before does not of itself make them an expert.
- o What is the expert's academic background, experience in the field, continuing professional development?
- o What training has the expert had in relation to being an expert witness?
- o Has the expert read Part 19 of the Criminal Procedure Rules? If not, ensure that they are provided with a copy.
- o Whether prosecuting or defending, is disclosure required under CrimPR 19.3(3)?
- o Has the expert read the Guidance Booklet for Experts? If not, and you are prosecuting, ensure that they are provided with a copy.
- o Which courts has the expert given evidence in before?
- o When has the expert given evidence in the past?
- o Which party (prosecution or defence) has the expert previously been called by to give evidence?
- o Has the expert also given evidence in civil, family or international cases?
- o Has the expert signed a self-certificate, as set out in Appendix B of the Guidance Booklet for Experts?
- o Is there an unused material schedule specifically in relation to material relating to the expert's evidence?

- What contact, including email contact, has there been between the police or prosecutor and the expert?
- How regular has this contact been?
- Has the expert ever been precluded from giving evidence before? If so, when and in what circumstances?
- Has the expert given evidence on the same topic, which post-dates his statement or report? If so, did he make any concessions? If so, a new statement should be obtained setting out any relevant concessions that were made.
- If the prosecution and defence experts have met for the purposes of drawing up a list of issues in agreement and dispute, has a proper record of that meeting been kept? There should be no such thing as an, "off the record" meeting between experts.

CHAPTER NINE

THIRD-PARTY MATERIAL AND REDACTION

This chapter sets out the potential issues that may arise when relevant material is held, not by the prosecution, but by other organisations or individuals. We explore the obligations on the prosecution and the steps the defence themselves may take to secure disclosable material from third parties. Finally, we consider the issues that arise when documents are redacted.

The Attorney General's Guidelines on Disclosure (2022) sets out three 'steps' or 'principles' to consider on the topic of third-party material:

- Step 1: Establishing a Reasonable Line of Inquiry

- Step 2: Establishing Relevance

- Step 3: Balancing Rights

Step 1: Establishing a Reasonable Line of Inquiry

Paragraph 28 of the Attorney General's Guidelines states that, *"The CPIA Code and these guidelines make clear the obligation on the investigator to pursue all reasonable lines of inquiry in relation to any offence under investigation, its surrounding circumstances or any person being investigated. This requires the investigator to pursue all lines of inquiry whether they point towards or away from the suspect, that may reveal material* ***relevant*** *to the investigation or the likely issues at trial. This obligation is the same in respect of material held by third parties."*

Establishing a reasonable line of inquiry is not dependent on the defence indicating what the issues are in the case. The prosecution should not, for example, rely on a 'no comment' interview as an excuse not to consider whether a third party may hold material that is of assistance to the defence or may undermine the prosecution case. That said, reasonable lines of inquiry will be informed by any explanation that the defendant has provided in interview, in a defence statement or even at a pre-trial hearing such as the PTPH.

The defence can, therefore, assist with ensuring that the prosecution have considered third-party material by raising this issue in correspondence, at court and in the defence statement.

Step 2: Establishing Relevance

Whether there is in fact any potentially relevant third-party material will depend entirely on the particular issues in the case. As is stated in paragraph 30 of the Attorney General's Guidelines, *"It should never be assumed that because of the nature of an offence that is being investigated that particular types of material will need to be assessed. There will be cases where detailed scrutiny is needed. There must be a properly identifiable foundation for the inquiry, not mere conjecture or speculation."*

It is important to set out in the Disclosure Management Document any lines of enquiry pursued relating to third-party material. The DMD should set out the enquiries that have or have not been taken and the justification behind these decisions. This allows scrutiny at an early stage as to the whether such an approach is correct in all the circumstances of the case.

Paragraph 32 of the Attorney General's Guidelines includes a helpful, non-exhaustive, list of factors to consider when deciding whether third-party material should be requested:

> *"i. What relevant information is the material believed to contain?*

ii. Why is it believed that the material contains that relevant information? If it is likely that no relevant information will be contained within the material, a request should not be made.

iii. Will the request for the material intrude on a complainant's or witness's privacy?

iv. If the material requested does amount to an invasion of privacy, is it a proportionate and justifiable request to make in the circumstances of the individual case and any known issues? Consider vi. below or whether the information which may result in access amounting to an invasion of privacy can be redacted to remove anything that does not meet the disclosure test.

v. Depending on the stage of the case, does the material need to be obtained or would a request to preserve the material suffice until more information is known?

vi. Is there an alternative way of readily accessing the information such as open-source searches, searches of material obtained from the suspect, or speaking directly to a witness, that does not require a request to a third party?

vii. Consider the scope of the material required, for example are the entirety of an individual's medical records required or would a particular month or year be sufficient? Ensure the request is focused so that only relevant information is being sought.

viii. The process of disclosure and its role in the justice system should be clearly and understandably expressed to the third party. They must be kept appraised of any ongoing disclosure decisions that are made with regard to their material."

Step 3: Balancing Rights

Paragraph 33 of the Attorney General's Guidelines emphasises that third party material, *"may reveal intimate, personal or delicate information. Prosecutors should give close scrutiny to such material and only disclose it where absolutely necessary."*

There can arise a real conflict between a victim of crime's Article 8 right to privacy and a defendant's Article 6 right to a fair trial. Where such a conflict arises, this must be resolved in favour of the defendant. Further guidance is set out in paragraphs 12 and 13 of the Attorney General's Guidelines:

> *"12. Fulfilling disclosure obligations is part of ensuring a fair trial in accordance with Article 6 of the ECHR. To comply with Article 6, during the course of an investigation, the investigator or prosecutor may decide that it is necessary to request and/or process personal or private information from a complainant or witness to pursue a reasonable line of inquiry; this includes, but is not limited to, digital material.*
>
> *13. When seeking to obtain and review such material, investigators and prosecutors should be aware that these lines of inquiry may engage that individual's Article 8 rights and those rights in respect of other parties within that material. Such material may also include sensitive data. When seeking to satisfy their disclosure obligations in these circumstances, investigators and prosecutors should apply the following principles:*
>
> *a. Collecting and/or processing personal or private material can only be done when in accordance with the law, strictly necessary, and proportionate.*
>
> *b. In order to be in accordance with the law and necessary, an investigator must be pursuing a reasonable line of inquiry in seeking to obtain the material. What constitutes a reasonable line of inquiry may be informed by others, including the prosecutor and the defendant.*

Seeking the personal or private information of a complainant or witness will not be a reasonable line of inquiry in every case – an assessment of reasonableness is required…

c. The assessment of reasonableness must be made on a case-by-case basis and regard may be had to:

(i) the prospect of obtaining relevant material; and

(ii) what the perceived relevance of that material is, having regard to the identifiable facts and issues in the individual case;

d. If by following a reasonable line of inquiry, it becomes necessary to obtain personal or private material, investigators will also need to consider:

(i) what review is required;

(ii) how the review of this material should be conducted;

(iii) what is the least intrusive method which will nonetheless secure relevant material;

(iv) are particular parameters for searching best suited to the identification of relevant material;

(v) is provision of the material in its entirety to the investigator strictly necessary; or alternatively, could the material be obtained from other sources, or by the investigator viewing and/or capturing the material in situ? An incremental approach should be taken to the degree of intrusion.

e. The rationale for pursuing the reasonable line of inquiry and the scope of the review it necessitates should be open and transparent. It should be capable of articulation by the investigator making the decision. It should provide the basis for:

(i) consultation with the prosecutor,

(ii) engagement with the defence and,

(iii) the provision of information to the witness about how their material is to be handled.

f. The refusal by a witness to provide private or personal material requires an investigator and prosecutor to consider the information the witness has been provided (and could be provided) with regard to the use of their personal material, the reasons for refusal, and how the trial process could address the absence of the material.

g. Disclosure of such material to the defence is in accordance with the law and necessary if, but only if, the material meets the disclosure test in the CPIA 1996. Personal information which does not meet this test but is contained within the material to be disclosed should be redacted.

h. Where there is a conflict between both of these rights, investigators and prosecutors should bear in mind that the right to a fair trial is an absolute right. Where prosecutors and investigators work within the framework provided by the CPIA, any unavoidable intrusion into privacy rights is likely to be justified, so long as any intrusion is no more than necessary."

An example of where a conflict between a victim's Article 8 right to privacy and the defendant's Article 6 right to a fair trial might arise is in relation to pre-trial therapy notes. This is the subject of specific CPS Guidance on 'Pre-Trial Therapy' (26 May 2022), which also emphasises the need to communicate the prosecution's approach in the Disclosure Management Document.

Another example where a conflict between the right to privacy and the right to a fair trial might arise is the extent to which police obtain material from a complainant's mobile phone or social media. That would, of course, depend on the nature of the allegation, the period of time over which the offence is said to have taken place and whether the complainant and defendant had met or communicated before the alleged offence.

One practical way of balancing rights in the disclosure process is to redact as far as possible any personal data which does not need to be disclosed. Redaction is considered further at the end of this chapter.

Duty to pursue all reasonable lines of enquiry

The investigator in any case has a duty to pursue all reasonable lines of enquiry. Paragraphs 3.5 and 3.6 of the CPIA Code of Practice (2020) provide the following guidance:

> *"3.5 In conducting an investigation, the investigator should pursue all reasonable lines of inquiry, whether these point towards or away from the suspect. What is reasonable in each case will depend on the particular circumstances. It is a matter for the investigator, with the assistance of the prosecutor if required, to decide what constitutes a reasonable line of inquiry in each case.*
>
> *3.6 If the officer in charge of an investigation believes that other persons may be in possession of material that may be relevant to the investigation, and if this has not been obtained under paragraph 3.5 above, they should ask the disclosure officer to inform them of the existence of the investigation and to invite them to retain the material in case they receive a request for its disclosure. The disclosure officer should inform the prosecutor that they may have such material. However, the officer in charge of an investigation is not required to make speculative enquiries of other persons; there must be some reason to believe that they may have relevant material. That reason may come from information provided to the police by the accused or from other inquiries made or from some other source."*

Material held by Government departments

The correct approach to obtaining relevant material from Government departments is covered by paragraphs 35-40 of the Attorney General's Guidelines. In particular, note paragraphs 39-40, which provide as follows,

> *"39. Investigators and prosecutors cannot be regarded to be in constructive possession of material held by Government departments or Crown bodies simply by virtue of their status as Government departments or Crown bodies.*
>
> *40. The steps taken to identify and obtain relevant material held by a Government department or Crown body should be recorded by the investigator and the prosecutor.*
>
> *41. Where appropriate, the defence should be informed of the steps taken to obtain material and the results of the line of inquiry."*

Witness summons

Paragraph 43 of the Attorney General's Guidelines states,

> *"43. If access to the material is refused and, despite the reasons given for refusal of access, it is still believed that it is reasonable to seek production of the material or information and that the requirements of a witness summons are satisfied (or any other relevant power), then the prosecutor or investigator should apply for the summons causing a representative of the third party to produce the material to court. A witness summons is only available once a case has been charged. If the material is sought pre-charge, investigators and prosecutors should request that the third party preserve the material. This request should be documented."*

The criteria for applying for a witness summons is set out in section 2 of the *Criminal Procedure (Attendance of Witnesses) Act* 1965 and is drafted in similar terms to section 97 of the *Magistrates' Court Act* 1980. Section 2 states:

> "**2.— Issue of witness summons on application to Crown Court.**
>
> *(1) This section applies where the Crown Court is satisfied that—*
>
> *(a) a person is likely to be able to give evidence likely to be material evidence, or produce any document or thing likely to be material evidence, for the purpose of any criminal proceedings before the Crown Court, and*
>
> *(b) it is in the interests of justice to issue a summons under this section to secure the attendance of that person to give evidence or to produce the document or thing.*
>
> *(2) In such a case the Crown Court shall, subject to the following provisions of this section, issue a summons (a witness summons) directed to the person concerned and requiring him to—*
>
> *(a) attend before the Crown Court at the time and place stated in the summons, and*
>
> *(b) give the evidence or produce the document or thing.*
>
> *(3) A witness summons may only be issued under this section on an application; and the Crown Court may refuse to issue the summons if any requirement relating to the application is not fulfilled…*"

Section 2A of the *Criminal Procedure (Attendance of Witnesses) Act* 1965 states:

> ***"2A Power to require advance production.***
>
> *A witness summons which is issued under section 2 above and which requires a person to produce a document or thing as mentioned in*

section 2(2) above may also require him to produce the document or thing—

(a) at a place stated in the summons, and

(b) at a time which is so stated and precedes that stated under section 2(2) above,

for inspection by the person applying for the summons"

When applying for a witness summons, regard should also be made to Part 17 of the Criminal Procedure Rules, which sets out the procedural requirements in relation to applying for witness summonses, warrants or orders. In particular, CrimPR 17.5 and 17.6 state:

"17.5.—(1) This rule applies to an application under rule 17.3 for a witness summons requiring the proposed witness—

(a) to produce in evidence a document or thing; or

(b) to give evidence about information apparently held in confidence,

that relates to another person.

(2) The application must be in writing in the form required by rule 17.4.

(3) The party applying must serve the application—

(a) on the proposed witness, unless the court otherwise directs; and

(b) on one or more of the following, if the court so directs—

(i) a person to whom the proposed evidence relates,

(ii) another party.

(4) The court must not issue a witness summons where this rule applies unless—

(a) everyone served with the application has had at least 10 business days in which to make representations, including representations about whether there should be a hearing of the application before the summons is issued; and

(b) the court is satisfied that it has been able to take adequate account of the duties and rights, including rights of confidentiality, of the proposed witness and of any person to whom the proposed evidence relates.

(5) This rule does not apply to an application for an order to produce in evidence a copy of an entry in bank records.

17.6.—(1) This rule applies where a person served with an application for a witness summons requiring the proposed witness to produce in evidence a document or thing objects to its production on the ground that—

(a) it is not likely to be material evidence; or

(b) even if it is likely to be material evidence, the duties or rights, including rights of confidentiality, of the proposed witness or of any person to whom the document or thing relates, outweigh the reasons for issuing a summons.

(2) The court may require the proposed witness to make the document or thing available for the objection to be assessed.

(3) The court may invite—

(a) the proposed witness or any representative of the proposed witness; or

> *(b) a person to whom the document or thing relates or any representative of such a person,*
>
> *to help the court assess the objection."*

In *R v Alibhai* [2004] EWCA Crim 681, Longmore LJ, commenting on the process of applying for a witness summons, stated at paragraph 34,

> *"... This procedure is not altogether satisfactory because:—*
>
> *(a) it is impossible to issue a witness summons to a person outside the jurisdiction;*
>
> *(b) a witness summons to produce a "document or thing" will not elicit information;*
>
> *(c) the "document or thing" must itself be likely to be material evidence; a witness summons will not be issued for documents which will not themselves constitute evidence in the case but merely give rise to a line of enquiry which might result in evidence being obtained, still less for documents merely capable of use in cross-examination as to credit;*
>
> *(d) there is no provision for either the Crown or the defence, in the absence of agreement, to examine the documents before they are produced to the court pursuant to the witness summons..."*

If the prosecution do not apply for a witness summons, the defence should consider doing so. This was clearly envisaged in paragraphs 44 and 48 of the Judicial Protocol on the Disclosure of Unused Material in Criminal Cases (2013):

> *"44. Where material is held by a third party such as a local authority, a social services department, hospital or business, the investigators and the prosecution may need to make enquiries of the third party, with a view to inspecting the material and assessing whether the relevant test for disclosure is met and determining whether any or all of the material*

should be retained, recorded and, in due course, disclosed to the accused. If access by the prosecution is granted, the investigators and the prosecution will need to establish whether the custodian of the material intends to raise PII issues, as a result of which the material may have to be placed before the court for a decision. ***This does not obviate the need for the defence to conduct its own enquiries as appropriate.*** *Speculative enquiries without any proper basis in relation to third party material – whether by the prosecution or the defence – are to be discouraged, and, in appropriate cases, the court will consider making an order for costs where an application is clearly unmeritorious and misconceived.*

...

48. The judge should consider whether to take any steps if a third party fails, or refuses, to comply with a request for disclosure, including suggesting that either of the parties pursue the request and, if necessary, make an application for a witness summons. In these circumstances, the court will need to set an appropriate timetable .... Any failure to comply with the timetable must immediately be referred back to the court for further directions, although a hearing will not always be necessary. ***Generally, it may be appropriate for the defence to pursue requests of this kind when the prosecution, for good reason, decline to do so and the court will need to ensure that this procedure does not delay the trial.***" (emphasis added)

PTPH form

There are specific sections of the Plea & Trial Preparation Hearing form that address Third-Party Disclosure. Please see pages 2, 3, 9, 10 and 11 of the PTPH form, a copy of which is set out at the end of **Chapter Three.**

Cases involving children

No evidence or document in family proceedings or information about the proceedings should be disclosed into criminal proceedings without the leave of the Family Court. The case of *Re C (A Minor) (Care Proceedings: Disclosure)* [1997] 2 WLR 322, [1997] Fam. 76 also reported as *Re EC (Disclosure of Material)* [1996] 2 FLR 725 sets out factors for the court to consider when deciding whether to disclose information:

> *"In the light of the authorities, the following are among the matters which a judge will consider when deciding whether to order disclosure. It is impossible to place them in any order of importance, because the importance of each of the various factors will inevitably vary very much from case to case.*
>
> *(1) The welfare and interests of the child or children concerned in the care proceedings. If the child is likely to be adversely affected by the order in any serious way, this will be a very important factor.*
>
> *(2) The welfare and interests of other children generally.*
>
> *(3) The maintenance of confidentiality in children cases.*
>
> *(4) The importance of encouraging frankness in children's cases. All parties to this appeal agree that this is a very important factor and is likely to be of particular importance in a case to which section 98(2) applies. The underlying purpose of section 98 is to encourage people to tell the truth in cases concerning children, and the incentive is that any admission will not be admissible in evidence in a criminal trial. Consequently, it is important in this case. However, the added incentive of guaranteed confidentiality is not given by the words of the section and cannot be given.*

(5) The public interest in the administration of justice. Barriers should not be erected between one branch of the judicature and another because this may be inimical to the overall interests of justice.

(6) The public interest in the prosecution of serious crime and the punishment of offenders, including the public interest in convicting those who have been guilty of violent or sexual offences against children. There is a strong public interest in making available material to the police which is relevant to a criminal trial. In many cases, this is likely to be a very important factor.

(7) The gravity of the alleged offence and the relevance of the evidence to it. If the evidence has little or no bearing on the investigation or the trial, this will militate against a disclosure order.

(8) The desirability of co-operation between various agencies concerned with the welfare of children, including the social services departments, the police service, medical practitioners, health visitors, schools, etc. This is particularly important in cases concerning children.

(9) In a case to which section 98(2) applies, the terms of the section itself, namely that the witness was not excused from answering incriminating questions, and that any statement of admission would not be admissible against him in criminal proceedings. Fairness to the person who has incriminated himself and any others affected by the incriminating statement and any danger of oppression would also be relevant considerations.

(10) Any other material disclosure which has already taken place."

In *Re M (Children)(Disclosure to the Police)* [2019] EWCA Civ 1364, the Court of Appeal stated that applications for disclosure should only be granted if the criteria in *Re C* are satisfied and it is necessary and proportionate to do so.

It is also worth noting that page 9 of the PTPH form contains a draft order that,

> *"Prosecution to make any application required to the Family Court by…"*

Please see PTPH form at the end of **Chapter Three**.

Reference should also be made to the '2013 Protocol and Good Practice Model: Disclosure of information in cases of alleged child abuse and linked criminal and care directions hearings'. This is available online at:

https://www.judiciary.uk/wp-content/uploads/JCO/Documents/Guidance/protocol-good-practice-model-2013.pdf

This Protocol was agreed on 17 October 2013 and signed by the Senior Presiding Judge for England and Wales, the President of the Family Division and the Director of Public Prosecutions. Part B of the Protocol provides a framework for disclosure from the Local Authority / Family Justice System into the Criminal Justice System, and covers the following topics:

> *"8. Notification by local authority to the police of the existence and status of family proceedings*
>
> *9. Police request to local authority for disclosure*
>
> *10. Disclosure by the local authority to the police*
>
> *11. Applications by police and the CPS to the family court for disclosure of material relating to family proceedings*
>
> *12. Text or summary of judgment in family proceedings*
>
> *13. Disclosure by the CPS to the criminal defence*
>
> *14. Public Interest Immunity (PII) Application"*

In particular, the following sections within Part B deal with applications to the Family Court for disclosure:

> *"11.1. At the stage prior to service of prosecution papers pursuant to section 51 of the Crime and Disorder Act 1998, applications will be generally made by the police. After this stage, applications will generally be made by the CPS.*
>
> *11.2. Applications by the police for disclosure must contain details of the named officer to whom release is sought and must specify the purpose and use to which the material is intended to be put. Applications should seek leave (where appropriate) to disclose the material to the CPS, to disclose the material to the criminal defence solicitors and (subject to section 98(2) of the Children Act 1989) to use the material in evidence at the criminal proceedings.*
>
> *11.3. Applications by the CPS must specify the purpose and use to which the material is intended to be put and should seek leave to share the material with the police and with the defence and (subject to section 98(2) Children Act 1989) to use the material in evidence at the criminal proceedings.*
>
> *11.4. Applications shall be made on Form C2. The application must be served by police or the CPS on all Parties to the Family Proceedings (The Local Authority having informed the police of details of all parties to Family Proceedings as per paragraphs 8.1 and 8.2 of this protocol).*
>
> *11.5. The application will be determined at a hearing at the Family Court. Police and the CPS will not attend the hearing unless directed to do so by the Family Court."*

The following sections of the Protocol are also worth noting in relation to when an application for a witness summons may be required and where PII is sought on the basis of lack of consent from the person to whom the confidential document relates:

"10.7. Where, in exceptional circumstances, the Local Authority is not able to include other material (not relating to Family Court proceedings) in the files to be examined by the police, the Local Authority will notify the police in writing of the existence of this material; indicating the reason why the material is not being made available to the police. Such a course should be exceptional because the Local Authority recognises that the material will be regarded as sensitive by the police and the CPS. It will not be disclosed to the defence without further consultation with the Local Authority or order of the court...

13.7. Where in accordance with paragraph 10.7 above a Local Authority document is not made available to the police on the basis of confidentiality (e.g. consent has not been obtained from the person to whom the document relates), the CPS will consider whether it is appropriate to seek access to such material by means of a witness summons in the criminal court.

13.8. Where in these circumstances application is made by the CPS for a witness summons, the CPS will serve the application on the criminal court and the Local Authority, identifying the Local Authority SPOC ['Single Point of Contact'] *as the person who is required to produce the document(s). In addition, where the Crown Court so directs, the CPS will, in accordance with the Criminal Procedure Rules, serve the application on the person to whom the confidential document relates.*

14.3. Where PII is sought on the basis of lack of consent from the person to whom the confidential document relates, CPS must in accordance with the Criminal Procedure Rules notify the person to whom the document relates (as above, notification of date and venue of PII application and the interested person's right to make representations to the court)."

International Third Parties

In some cases, a third party may be outside the jurisdiction. The prosecution are still, however, obliged to take reasonable steps to obtain relevant material from abroad. Paragraphs 59-63 of the Attorney General's Guidelines state,

> *"59. The obligations under the CPIA Code to pursue all reasonable lines of enquiry apply to material held overseas.*
>
> *60. Where it appears that there is relevant material, the prosecutor must take reasonable steps to obtain it, either informally or making use of the powers contained in the Crime (International Co-operation) Act 2003 and any EU and international conventions. See CPS Guidance 'Obtaining Evidence and Information from Abroad'.*
>
> *61. There may be cases where a foreign state or a foreign court refuses to make the material available to the investigator or prosecutor. There may be other cases where the foreign state, though willing to show the material to investigators, will not allow the material to be copied or otherwise made available and the courts of the foreign state will not order its provision.*
>
> *62. It is for these reasons that there is no absolute duty on the prosecutor to disclose relevant material held overseas by entities not subject to the jurisdiction of the courts in England and Wales. However consideration should be given to whether the type of material believed to be held can be provided to the defence.*
>
> *63. The obligation on the investigator and prosecutor under the CPIA is to take reasonable steps. Where investigators are allowed to examine files of a foreign state but are not allowed to take copies or notes or list the documents held, there is no breach by the prosecution in its duty of disclosure by reason of its failure to obtain such material, provided reasonable steps have been taken to try and obtain the material.* ***Prosecutors have a margin of consideration as to what steps are***

appropriate in the particular case but prosecutors must be alive to their duties and there may be some circumstances where these duties cannot be met. *Whether the prosecutor has taken reasonable steps is for the court to determine in each case if the matter is raised." (emphasis added)*

In *R v Flook* [2009] EWCA Crim 682; [2010] 1 Cr. App. R. 30, the Court of Appeal also gave guidance on the prosecution's disclosure obligations in relation to obtaining relevant material from abroad:

> *"32. The general duties of the Crown, whether through the police, other investigating agency or the prosecutor, in relation to disclosure in criminal proceedings are set out in the CPIA, as amended. However the CPIA makes no special provision in relation to material held by individuals or companies overseas or by foreign governmental authorities or material that may be examined overseas in the course of the investigation…*
>
> *34. In R v Alibhai [2004] EWCA Crim 681, this court considered the Crown's disclosure obligation in respect of material in the possession of a US company and the FBI who had been assisting the prosecution and had produced a considerable amount of material…*
>
>> *'63. … the prosecutor is not under an absolute obligation to secure the disclosure of the material or information. He enjoys what might be described as a "margin of consideration" as to what steps he regards as appropriate in the particular case. If criticism is to be made of a failure to secure third party disclosure, it would have to be shown that the prosecutor did not act within the permissible limits afforded by the Guidelines.*
>>
>> *64. In saying this, we are not ruling out the possibility that in an extreme case it might be so unfair for a prosecution to proceed in the absence of material which a third party declines to produce that it would be proper to stay it, regardless of whether the prosecutor is in breach of the Guidelines. … However, in so far as [the appellant],*

suggests that the trial was unfair because of breach of the Guidelines, it is important to bear in mind the limits upon what was required of the prosecutor under the Guidelines.'

35. The 2005 Guidelines are more prescriptive than the 2000 Guidelines and the obligation of the Crown more explicit. In our view, the provisions of the Code and the 2005 Guidelines, although expressed in a domestic context, make clear the obligation of the Crown (whether investigator or prosecutor) is to pursue reasonable lines of enquiry in relation to material that may be held overseas in states outside the European Union; we do not deal with the position of material within states of the European Union as the legal regime is different. If it appears that there is relevant material, then the Crown must take reasonable steps to obtain it, either informally or making use of the powers contained in the Crime (International Co-operation) Act 2003 and international conventions...

36. However, it is self evident that where there may be material relevant in that sense overseas outside the European Union, the power of the Crown and the courts of England and Wales to obtain material is limited. Essentially, if informal requests for the material are declined, the powers are limited to what is set out in the Crime (International Co-operation) Act 2003 and in relevant international conventions, such as the Drugs Convention. There may be cases where a foreign entity will simply not make the material available, a foreign court will not compel production under a Letter of Request and steps under the relevant convention will not produce the documents. There may be other cases where the authorities of a foreign state, though willing to show material to officers acting on behalf of the United Kingdom, will not allow the material to be copied or otherwise made available and the courts of the foreign state will not order its provision.

37. There cannot, for these reasons, be any absolute obligation on the Crown to disclose relevant material held overseas outside the European Union by entities not subject to the jurisdiction of these courts; the position is quite different to the position where the information is held in the United Kingdom or by a person amenable to the jurisdiction of these courts. As Sir Igor Judge said in R v Khyam [2008] EWCA Crim 1612 at paragraph 37:

> *'The prosecuting authorities in this jurisdiction simply cannot compel authorities in a foreign country to acknowledge, let alone comply with, our disclosure principles.'*

The obligation is one to take reasonable steps. Whether the Crown has complied with that obligation is for the courts to judge in each case on the provision of full information to the court. It is not necessary for us to decide whether the Crown any longer has the margin of consideration referred to in Alibhai."

Mutual Legal Assistance

Mutual Legal Assistance is defined in the Home Office's 'Request for Mutual Legal Assistance in Criminal Matters – Guidelines for Authorities outside of the United Kingdom' (2022) as follows:

> *"Mutual Legal Assistance (MLA) is a method of cooperation between States for obtaining assistance in the investigation of criminal offences. MLA is generally used for obtaining material that cannot be obtained on a law enforcement to law enforcement basis...particularly enquiries that require coercive measures. Requests are made by a formal International Letter of Request (ILOR or LOR), also known as Commissions Rogatoires in civil law jurisdictions. This assistance is usually requested by courts or prosecutors and is therefore also referred to as 'judicial cooperation'."*

These Home Office Guidelines provide useful assistance in relation to the practice and procedure for making requests for material held abroad. It should be noted, however, that since the United Kingdom's withdrawal from the EU on 31 January 2020, a European Investigation Order ('EIO') can no longer be issued to obtain evidence located in EU Member States for use in UK criminal investigations or proceedings.

In practice, therefore, responses to requests to foreign jurisdictions, including to any EU Member State, can take a significant amount of time. In an appropriate case, therefore, in order to demonstrate that the prosecution have pursued all reasonable lines of enquiry, they will need to demonstrate that they have made their enquiries expeditiously and also chased up those enquiries.

In summary, therefore, the prosecution must pursue all reasonable lines of enquiry, including those which point away from the defendant's guilt or which may otherwise assist the defence. That obligation extends to material that may be in the hands of third parties, even if those third parties are outside the jurisdiction. The defence too have a role to play in certain circumstances to conduct their own enquiries and to pursue applications for disclosure from third parties.

We set out below a brief checklist, which may assist when considering disclosure from third parties.

THIRD PARTY CHECKLIST

- What directions did the court give at the PTPH in relation to third-party material?
- Have the prosecution given consideration to the existence of third-party material?
- Have all third-party enquiries been completed?
- If not, what is the timeframe for the completion of third-party enquiries?
- Is this timeframe realistic or might it have an impact on the trial date?
- Is it necessary to seek a court order to ensure the production of third-party material?
- Have the prosecution set out their approach to third-party material in a Disclosure Management Document?
- If the defence disagree with the prosecution's approach, have they raised their objections or concerns with the prosecution and/or the court?
- Have the defence referred the prosecution to the existence of third-party material?
- Have the defence, themselves, taken steps to obtain third-party material?

REDACTION

From the prosecution perspective, care must be take not to over redact material (evidence or disclosure). From the defence point of view, a healthy scepticism is advisable when provided with documents that have been redacted.

Where necessary and proportionate, the police will redact material that they provide to the CPS to allow a charging decision to be made. In turn, the CPS may subsequently apply additional redactions to documents before they are served in evidence or disclosed to the defence.

Annex D of the Attorney General's Guidelines on Disclosure (2022) provides specific guidance in relation to the redaction decision-making process. Annex D refers to this process as, *"any way of obscuring personal data, including but not limited to redaction, clipping, pixelization, anonymisation or pseudonymisation"*.

Whilst Annex D is aimed at material that is provided to the prosecutor at the charging decision stage, it contains a number of very helpful principles with which to assess whether the correct approach to redacting material has been adopted.

When documents are redacted before they are disclosed, this should be done in such a way that makes it clear to the reader that the document has actually been edited; for example,

> "John Self resides at ████████████████████ and can be contacted on ██████████ ."

In addition, thought should be given, where appropriate, to adding a gist to any passages in a document that have been redacted, to inform the reader as to the nature of the material that has been obscured. So, instead of disclosing documents which may contain paragraphs or indeed pages that have been entirely blacked out, it may assist to add at least some description, for example, "[Provides details of children's names, dates of birth and school.]" or "[Details of a health condition.]"

Set out below are extracts from Annex D, which gives a framework of principles which the prosecution should use to guide any use of redactions.

Personal data

Annex D states:

> *"2. Providing data to the CPS or any other party from the police is an action regulated by data protection law. There may be a number of reasons why data is processed: if it is for law enforcement purposes it will fall under the Data Protection Act 2018, Part 3; otherwise, it may fall within the UK GDPR and other parts of the DPA 2018."*
>
> *"8. Personal data is information which relates to an identified or identifiable individual. If the data is not personal data, it will not need redacting for UK GDPR/DPA 2018 reasons (there may be other grounds for redaction such as sensitivity).*
>
> *9. Where the information is personal data, but the person does not have a reasonable expectation of privacy, it will not need to be redacted.*
>
> *a. Typically, helicopter or drone footage of people in public locations, vehicle registrations on public roads, staff and customers in shops and openly recorded interviews of witnesses would not likely fall to be redacted.*
>
> *b. Typically, covert recordings, recordings in a domestic setting or footage of other persons detained at a police station would likely fall to be redacted."*

Applying the Necessity Test

Annex D states:

"10. Where the data is relevant, personal and there is a reasonable expectation of privacy, investigators will need to go on to consider whether it is nonetheless necessary or strictly necessary to provide it to the CPS in an unredacted form for the purposes of making a charging decision. Where it is necessary or strictly necessary to do so, the data need not be redacted; where data does not meet this standard, it should be redacted.

...

11. Necessity tests are a balancing exercise, the reasons in favour of disclosing must outweigh those against. This balance should be assessed objectively and on a case-by-case basis. The purpose of the data being used must always be at the centre of any decision. Whether the test is of necessity or strict necessity will not change this approach. However, a strict necessity standard requires a greater evidential basis to justify providing the data unredacted.

- *'Necessity' has its natural meaning. It does not mean there is absolutely no other possible option. Investigators must balance the rights of the individual(s) involved with the legitimate public interest in an informed charging decision.*

- *Strict necessity' is a higher standard than necessary and applies to sensitive personal data. Data about criminal convictions and offences is sensitive and so is any data which is categorised as sensitive by the UK GDPR. This is:*

i. personal data revealing racial or ethnic origin;

ii. personal data revealing political opinions;

iii. personal data revealing religious or philosophical beliefs;

iv. personal data revealing trade union membership;

v. genetic data;

vi. biometric data (where used for identification purposes);

vii. data concerning health;

viii. data concerning a person's sex life; and

ix. data concerning a person's sexual orientation."

Balancing rights

Annex D states:

"12. When deciding whether data is necessary or strictly necessary to provide unredacted, investigators should take into consideration the balance of rights and legitimate need.

- *The greater the expectation of privacy over the data, the more likely it is to require redaction.*

  - *For example, greater consideration will likely need to be given to whether to provide medical or financial data unredacted than names or dates of birth.*

- *The greater the detriment to a person if their privacy is not maintained, the more likely it is to require redaction.*

  - *For example, information which is of an intimate or revealing nature will need greater consideration than that which is not.*

- *The greater the value of the data to the function being undertaken, the less likely it is to require redaction.*

- *For example, the date of birth of a person in a prosecution may be critical (e.g. to proving an offence where the prosecution must show the victim was under a certain age), important (e.g. to illustrate the relative age of two persons in the case) or of no apparent importance…"*

The application of redactions should, therefore, be scrutinised to ensure that they do not obscure potentially disclosable material, such as a key address, the name of a potential eye witness, or important context in relation to other material that has been served in evidence or disclosed.

The defence should not hesitate to ask the prosecutor to justify why redactions have been applied. It may be helpful to remind the prosecutor of the continuing obligation on an accused to keep disclosed material confidential by virtue of section 17 of the CPIA, which we set out in **Chapter Three.** Section 17 may, therefore, act as a reassurance to a prosecutor who has concerns of material or information being disseminated to a wider audience.

If necessary, the defence should consider making a written request for redactions to be lifted and, if those requests are refused, inviting the prosecution to justify to the court why particular redactions have been applied.

CHAPTER TEN

PII APPLICATIONS

Another category of unused material is sensitive material. Although the defence do not receive the schedule of sensitive material, the MG6D, they will usually be alerted if there is to be a Public Interest Immunity ('PII') application.

Section 3(6) of the CPIA states that,

> *"Material must not be disclosed under this section to the extent that the court, on an application by the prosecutor, concludes it is not in the public interest to disclose it and orders accordingly."*

Section 15 of the CPIA states that,

> *"...(3) The court must keep under review the question whether at any given time it is still not in the public interest to disclose material affected by its order.*
>
> *(4) The court must keep the question mentioned in subsection (3) under review without the need for an application; but the accused may apply to the court for a review of that question.*
>
> *(5) If the court at any time concludes that it is in the public interest to disclose material to any extent—*
>
> *(a) it shall so order, and*
>
> *(b) it shall take such steps as are reasonable to inform the prosecutor of its order.*

> *(6) Where the prosecutor is informed of an order made under subsection (5) he must act accordingly having regard to the provisions of this Part (unless he decides not to proceed with the case concerned)."*

Section 14 of the CPIA provides a similar provision in the case of summary trials, albeit that section does not specify that the court must keep the question of PII under review regardless of whether an application for a review is made.

R v H

Lord Bingham of Cornhill explained the PII application process in *R v H and others* [2004] UKHL 3, [2004] 2 AC 134 as follows:

> *"18. Circumstances may arise in which material held by the prosecution and tending to undermine the prosecution or assist the defence cannot be disclosed to the defence, fully or even at all, without the risk of serious prejudice to an important public interest. The public interest most regularly engaged is that in the effective investigation and prosecution of serious crime, which may involve resort to informers and undercover agents, or the use of scientific or operational techniques (such as surveillance) which cannot be disclosed without exposing individuals to the risk of personal injury or jeopardising the success of future operations. In such circumstances some derogation from the golden rule of full disclosure may be justified but such derogation must always be the minimum derogation necessary to protect the public interest in question and must never imperil the overall fairness of the trial.*
>
> *19. The English law of crown privilege, later public interest immunity ("PII"), was largely developed in civil cases. This was because, before and even after the Attorney General's 1981 Guidelines, disclosure was left largely to the judgment of the prosecuting authorities and the prosecution and only exceptionally did the court make any ruling. Thus the defence were commonly unaware of what had not been disclosed*

and there was no judicial decision against which a defendant could appeal.

20. The shortcomings of this unsatisfactory regime were vividly exposed by the Court of Appeal's ground-breaking decision in R v Ward [1993] 1 WLR 619 , to which reference has already been made. The effect of the judgment was to require the prosecution, if it sought to claim PII for documents helpful to the defence, to give notice of the claim to the defence so that, if necessary, the court could be asked to rule on the legitimacy of the prosecution's asserted claim... The procedural implications of this judgment were refined by the Court of Appeal six months later in R v Davis [1993] 1 WLR 613. The court there distinguished between three classes of case... In the first, comprising most of the cases in which a PII issue arises, the prosecution must give notice to the defence that they are applying for a ruling of the court, and must indicate to the defence at least the category of the material they hold (that is, the broad ground upon which PII is claimed), and the defence must have the opportunity to make representations to the court. There is thus an inter partes hearing conducted in open court with reference to at least the category of the material in question. The second class comprises cases in which the prosecution contend that the public interest would be injured if disclosure were made even of the category of the material. In such cases the prosecution must still notify the defence that an application to the court is to be made, but the category of the material need not be specified: the defence will still have an opportunity to address the court on the procedure to be adopted but the application will be made to the court in the absence of the defendant or anyone representing him. If the court considers that the application falls within the first class, it will order that procedure to be followed. Otherwise it will rule. The third class, described as "highly exceptional", comprises cases where the public interest would be injured even by disclosure that an ex parte application is to be made. In such cases application to the court would be made without notice to the defence. But if the court considers that the case should be treated as falling within the second or the first class, it will so order. The court thus modified to a limited extent the ruling in R v Ward that notice of the making of an application should always be given to the defence..."

Lord Bingham went on to state,

"35. If material does not weaken the prosecution case or strengthen that of the defendant, there is no requirement to disclose it. For this purpose the parties' respective cases should not be restrictively analysed. But they must be carefully analysed, to ascertain the specific facts the prosecution seek to establish and the specific grounds on which the charges are resisted. The trial process is not well served if the defence are permitted to make general and unspecified allegations and then seek far-reaching disclosure in the hope that material may turn up to make them good. Neutral material or material damaging to the defendant need not be disclosed and should not be brought to the attention of the court. Only in truly borderline cases should the prosecution seek a judicial ruling on the disclosability of material in its hands. If the material contains information which the prosecution would prefer that the defendant did not have, on forensic as opposed to public interest grounds, that will suggest that the material is disclosable. If the disclosure test is faithfully applied, the occasions on which a judge will be obliged to recuse himself because he has been privately shown material damning to the defendant will, as the Court of Appeal envisaged ... be very exceptional indeed.

36. When any issue of derogation from the golden rule of full disclosure comes before it, the court must address a series of questions.

(1) What is the material which the prosecution seek to withhold? This must be considered by the court in detail.

(2) Is the material such as may weaken the prosecution case or strengthen that of the defence? If No, disclosure should not be ordered. If Yes, full disclosure should (subject to (3), (4) and (5) below) be ordered.

(3) Is there a real risk of serious prejudice to an important public interest (and, if so, what) if full disclosure of the material is ordered? If No, full disclosure should be ordered.

(4) If the answer to (2) and (3) is Yes, can the defendant's interest be protected without disclosure or disclosure be ordered to an extent or in a way which will give adequate protection to the public interest in question and also afford adequate protection to the interests of the defence?

This question requires the court to consider, with specific reference to the material which the prosecution seek to withhold and the facts of the case and the defence as disclosed, whether the prosecution should formally admit what the defence seek to establish or whether disclosure short of full disclosure may be ordered. This may be done in appropriate cases by the preparation of summaries or extracts of evidence, or the provision of documents in an edited or anonymised form, provided the documents supplied are in each instance approved by the judge. In appropriate cases the appointment of special counsel may be a necessary step to ensure that the contentions of the prosecution are tested and the interests of the defendant protected … In cases of exceptional difficulty the court may require the appointment of special counsel to ensure a correct answer to questions (2) and (3) as well as (4).

(5) Do the measures proposed in answer to (4) represent the minimum derogation necessary to protect the public interest in question? If No, the court should order such greater disclosure as will represent the minimum derogation from the golden rule of full disclosure.

(6) If limited disclosure is ordered pursuant to (4) or (5), may the effect be to render the trial process, viewed as a whole, unfair to the defendant? If Yes, then fuller disclosure should be ordered even if this leads or may lead the prosecution to discontinue the proceedings so as to avoid having to make disclosure.

(7) If the answer to (6) when first given is No, does that remain the correct answer as the trial unfolds, evidence is adduced and the defence advanced?

It is important that the answer to (6) should not be treated as a final, once-and-for-all, answer but as a provisional answer which the court must keep under review.

37. Throughout his or her consideration of any disclosure issue the trial judge must bear constantly in mind the overriding principles referred to in this opinion. In applying them, the judge should involve the defence to the maximum extent possible without disclosing that which the general interest requires to be protected but taking full account of the specific defence which is relied on. There will be very few cases indeed in which some measure of disclosure to the defence will not be possible, even if this is confined to the fact that an ex parte application is to be made. If even that information is withheld and if the material to be withheld is of significant help to the defendant, there must be a very serious question whether the prosecution should proceed, since special counsel, even if appointed, cannot then receive any instructions from the defence at all."

Rule 15.3 of the Criminal Procedure Rules

When making a PII application, reference should also be made to CrimPR 15.3, which states,

"Prosecutor's application for public interest ruling

***15.3.**—(1) This rule applies where—*

(a) without a court order, the prosecutor would have to disclose material; and

(b) the prosecutor wants the court to decide whether it would be in the public interest to disclose it.

(2) The prosecutor must—

(a) apply in writing for such a decision; and

(b) serve the application on—

(i) the court officer,

(ii) any person who the prosecutor thinks would be directly affected by disclosure of the material, and

(iii) the defendant, but only to the extent that serving it on the defendant would not disclose what the prosecutor thinks ought not be disclosed.

(3) The application must—

(a) describe the material, and explain why the prosecutor thinks that—

(i) it is material that the prosecutor would have to disclose,

(ii) it would not be in the public interest to disclose that material, and

(iii) no measure such as the prosecutor's admission of any fact, or disclosure by summary, extract or edited copy, adequately would protect both the public interest and the defendant's right to a fair trial;

(b) omit from any part of the application that is served on the defendant anything that would disclose what the prosecutor thinks ought not be disclosed (in which case, paragraph (4) of this rule applies); and

(c) explain why, if no part of the application is served on the defendant.

(4) Where the prosecutor serves only part of the application on the defendant, the prosecutor must—

(a) mark the other part, to show that it is only for the court; and

(b) in that other part, explain why the prosecutor has withheld it from the defendant.

(5) Unless already done, the court may direct the prosecutor to serve an application on—

(a) the defendant;

(b) any other person who the court considers would be directly affected by the disclosure of the material.

(6) The court must determine the application at a hearing which—

(a) must be in private, unless the court otherwise directs; and

(b) if the court so directs, may take place, wholly or in part, in the defendant's absence.

(7) At a hearing at which the defendant is present—

(a) the general rule is that the court must consider, in the following sequence—

(i) representations first by the prosecutor and any other person served with the application, and then by the defendant, in the presence of them all, and then

(ii) further representations by the prosecutor and any such other person in the defendant's absence; but

(b) the court may direct other arrangements for the hearing.

(8) The court may only determine the application if satisfied that it has been able to take adequate account of—

(a) such rights of confidentiality as apply to the material; and

(b) the defendant's right to a fair trial.

(9) Unless the court otherwise directs, the court officer—

(a) must not give notice to anyone other than the prosecutor—

(i) of the hearing of an application under this rule, unless the prosecutor served the application on that person, or

(ii) of the court's decision on the application;

(b) may—

(i) keep a written application or representations, or

(ii) arrange for the whole or any part to be kept by some other appropriate person, subject to any conditions that the court may impose."

Before a PII application is made, therefore, the defence can make representation to the trial judge. Such representations could include bringing the judge's attention to a particular part of the defence statement, or clarifying what the defendant's case is on a particular topic.

Importantly, the Criminal Procedure Rules also makes provision for the review of a court's decision to grant a PII application.

Rule 15.6 of the Criminal Procedure Rules

CrimPR 15.6 states,

"***15.6.***—*(1) This rule applies where the court has ordered that it is not in the public interest to disclose material that the prosecutor otherwise would have to disclose, and—*

(a) the defendant wants the court to review that decision; or

(b) the Crown Court reviews that decision on its own initiative.

(2) Where the defendant wants the court to review that decision, the defendant must—

(a) serve an application on—

(i) the court officer, and

(ii) the prosecutor; and

(b) in the application—

(i) describe the material that the defendant wants the prosecutor to disclose, and

(ii) explain why the defendant thinks it is no longer in the public interest for the prosecutor not to disclose it.

(3) The prosecutor must serve any such application on any person who the prosecutor thinks would be directly affected if that material were disclosed.

(4) The prosecutor, and any such person, must serve any representations on—

(a) the court officer; and

(b) the defendant, unless to do so would in effect reveal something that either thinks ought not be disclosed.

(5) The court may direct—

(a) the prosecutor to serve any such application on any person who the court considers would be directly affected if that material were disclosed;

(b) the prosecutor and any such person to serve any representations on the defendant.

(6) The court must review a decision to which this rule applies at a hearing which—

(a) must be in private, unless the court otherwise directs; and

(b) if the court so directs, may take place, wholly or in part, in the defendant's absence.

(7) At a hearing at which the defendant is present—

(a) the general rule is that the court must consider, in the following sequence—

(i) representations first by the defendant, and then by the prosecutor and any other person served with the application, in the presence of them all, and then

(ii) further representations by the prosecutor and any such other person in the defendant's absence; but

(b) the court may direct other arrangements for the hearing.

(8) The court may only conclude a review if satisfied that it has been able to take adequate account of—

(a) such rights of confidentiality as apply to the material; and

(b) the defendant's right to a fair trial."

Disclosure Manual: Annex C – Sensitive Material – Additional Guidance

Annex C of the CPS Disclosure Manual (Refreshed: 21 October 2021) provides practical advice in relation to preparing for a PII application. In relation to the PII hearing itself, Annex C states,

"When the judge's bundle has been provided to the court, the prosecutor should contact the court to ascertain whether the judge wishes to view the material giving rise to the application in advance of the hearing, or whether the court is content for the material to be brought to the hearing.

The prosecutor must make arrangements to facilitate inspection of all sensitive and highly sensitive material by the prosecution advocate well ahead of the hearing.

Where the judge requests sight of the material in advance of the hearing, the disclosure officer with responsibility for the material should make the necessary arrangements with the judge's clerk or court manager. There may need to be detailed discussions as to the handling and storage arrangements for the material when it is in the court's possession. In some circumstances, the police may wish to remain in the court building whilst the material is being considered so that they can recover it once the judge has viewed it. This will be a matter for local arrangements on a case-by-case basis.

The oral representations in support of the written submissions may be made by the reviewing prosecutor, CPS higher court advocate, the prosecution advocate, his/her junior or disclosure counsel. A CPS or departmental representative should be present at the hearing. The hearing should also be attended by the officer in charge of the investigation and all disclosure officers who have provided schedules listing items that are subject of the application.

The manner in which the hearing should be conducted will be a matter for the judge to determine. At a hearing at which the defendant is present, the general rule is that the court must consider representations first by the prosecutor and any other person served with the application, and then by the defendant, in the presence of them all, and then further representations by the prosecutor and any such other person in the defendant's absence.

The court may direct other arrangements for the hearing."

In any case involving a PII application, therefore, both prosecution and defence must ensure that the correct procedure is followed and that the application is justified.

Where the defence is on notice of a PII hearing, it may assist the judge if the defence, potentially with reference to the issues as set out in the defence statement, underscores the nature of the defence and the type of material that is considered disclosable and why immediately before the PII application is heard. The defence should also ensure that any PII ruling is kept under review as the trial progresses.

CHAPTER ELEVEN

PREVENTING DISCLOSURE PROBLEMS

In this chapter we set out some practical guidance, for both prosecution and defence advocates, to avoid getting into disclosure problems in the first place.

We have also included two checklists of questions that the practitioner may wish to use, depending on whether they are instructed to prosecute or defend. There is a natural overlap in these checklists. Often, problems arise from the fact that basic disclosure obligations have not been met; for example, on the first day of trial, the disclosure officer, usually the Officer in the Case (OIC), confirms they have not had sight of the defence statement. It is also not unheard of for a defendant at trial to dispute the content of his own defence statement, even if he has signed it, or for a defence statement to be served for the first time during the trial itself.

PROSECUTION PERSPECTIVE

The duty of prosecution advocates

A useful guide to the obligations on Prosecution Counsel can be found at paragraphs 135-138 of the Attorney General's Guidelines on Disclosure (2022):

> *"135. Prosecution advocates should ensure that all material which ought to be disclosed under the CPIA 1996 is disclosed to the defence. Prosecution advocates must ensure that they are fully informed about disclosure so that they are able to make decisions. Prosecution advocates must consider, in every case, whether they can be satisfied that they are*

in possession of all relevant documentation and that they have been fully instructed regarding disclosure matters. If the advocate considers that further information or action is required then written advice should be provided setting out the aspects that need clarification or action.

136. All decisions regarding disclosure must be kept under review until the conclusion of the trial, whenever possible in consultation with the reviewing prosecutor. The prosecution advocate must in every case specifically consider whether they can satisfactorily discharge the duty of continuing review on the basis of the material supplied already, or whether it is necessary to reconsider the unused material schedule and/or unused material.

137. Prosecution advocates must not abrogate their responsibility under the CPIA 1996 by disclosing material which does not pass the test for disclosure. This is especially so where it is proposed to disclose material engaging Article 8 rights.

138. There is no basis in practice or law for counsel-to-counsel disclosure. It is of critical importance that, even where prosecution counsel is advising and leading on disclosure, the duty to disclose material that meets the test for disclosure remains with the prosecutor. A record of material disclosed made must be kept, not least in the event of an appeal or a re-trial."

A prosecutor should not, therefore, disclose material to defence counsel on the condition that the material is not shown to her client. Defence practitioners must be mindful of the fact that there is no provision to view unused material on the understanding that it is not revealed to the client.

When counsel is instructed to prosecute, there will usually be particular instructions provided in relation to disclosure. These instructions are regularly amended and, by way of example may include addressing the quality of the DMD and confirming whether they are of the view that

that all reasonable lines of enquiry have been considered. Prosecution Counsel may also be asked to reconsider the reasonable lines on enquiry in light of the matters raised in the defence statemen and to assist with updating the DMD if that becomes necessary.

Aside from any specific instructions, it may be of assistance for the prosecution advocate to consider the following checklist. Although a number of the questions are more appropriate to larger and complex cases, we think that it will help to bear these points in mind to ensure that the disclosure process is fit for purpose. This checklist may, for example, be useful when holding a conference. Particular care should also be taken in cases where the defendant is unrepresented or a trial is proceeding in the defendant's absence.

PROSECUTION CHECKLIST

- What are the deadlines for initial disclosure, service of the defence statement, prosecution response to the defence statement, and any timetable relating to disclosure requests / section 8 applications and responses?
- Has an initial disclosure (section 3) letter been sent to the defence?
- Has a complete set of **all** the MG6Cs and accompanying MG6Es been provided with the brief?
- What is the date of the last MG6C?
- Are the MG6Cs complete, or is there more material still to be scheduled; for example, has there been any further material generated or identified since the date of the last MG6C but which is yet to be scheduled?
- If there is further unused material to be reviewed, when can this be done by and is there a danger that this will be too late for any court-imposed deadline or indeed the trial date?
- Are the descriptions on the MG6C clear and informative? If not, ask for clarification.
- Are all the MG6Cs signed and dated by the disclosure officer and reviewing lawyer?
- Have all entries been endorsed, for example CND, ND or D?
- Have all the items marked as disclosable actually been disclosed to the defence and provided to you?

- Do any items of evidence, for example witness statements, appear on the MG6C? If they do, and unless there is a note stating that the item has since been served as evidence, this may suggest that the disclosure officer did not know that a specific item is evidence instead of unused material. Ask for the OIC and disclosure officer to be provided with an index of the evidence that has been served on the defence.

- Have the MG6Cs been uploaded to the Digital Case System?

- Has a defence statement been served?

- Is the defence statement signed and dated?

- Does the defence statement identify the real issues in the case? If not, consider raising the adequacy of the defence statement with the defence and court.

- Has the disclosure officer provided signed and dated certification of the following: revelation of all relevant retained material; whether material satisfies the disclosure test; and whether material satisfies the disclosure test following a defence statement as part of the prosecution's continuing duty?

- Who is the disclosure officer?

- Is the disclosure officer different from the OIC?

- Has the disclosure officer seen a copy of the defence statement?

- Has there been a written response to the defence statement?

- Has a defence witness notice been served?

- Have the police conducted PNC checks (including where appropriate checks abroad) in relation to both prosecution and defence witnesses?
- Have there been any disclosure requests or section 8 applications and, if so, are any requests outstanding?
- Is there a signed, dated and endorsed MG6D? If so, ask to see a copy.
- Are the items described on the MG6C and MG6D on the correct schedules? For example, are there items on the MG6D that are not in fact sensitive and so should appear on an MG6C?
- Are there any outstanding enquiries?
- Are there any linked investigations?
- What third-party material is there?
- Is there any international material?
- Are there any ongoing international enquiries?
- If so, when are they expected to be completed by?
- When was the decision made to pursue those enquiries?
- Is a Disclosure Record Sheet being completed by the CPS?
- Has a Disclosure Management Document been prepared?
- Do the police or investigating authority have a disclosure strategy document?

- Do the disclosure strategy and Disclosure Management Documents identify, (a) what the issues in the case are, and (b) set out the reasonable lines of enquiry that have been pursued?

- Has the Disclosure Management Document (DMD) been uploaded to the Digital Case System?

- Does there need to be any further Disclosure Management Documents drafted to cover specific disclosure issues?

- For cases involving Digital Material, please refer to the points raised in **Chapter Seven**.

- For cases involving expert witnesses, please refer to the checklist we have set out in **Chapter Eight**.

Adequacy of descriptions on the MG6C

One of the most important aspects of the disclosure exercise, is to ensure that items of unused material are properly described on the MG6C. In particular, in large and complex cases, advice may need to be given at an early stage to ensure that the quality and consistency of the descriptions are maintained.

Where there are large documents listed as individual items on the MG6C, for example files or folders of documents, the number of pages should be included in the description, where possible. In addition, if there are any disclosable pages within a larger folder of material, they should be split out and scheduled as separate items on the MG6C.

Where there are large documents, say in excess of 50 pages, where practicable, an index should be created and the index itself included as a separate item on the MG6C.

If a statement is an item on an MG6C it should always include the date or, if the statement is undated, that should also be recorded, so "Statement of X dated 31/07/2023..." or "Statement of X, undated...".

The description of exhibits, particularly electronic devices, on the MG6C should make the following clear in the description:

- What the item is, e.g. a mobile phone, a laptop, memory stick etc.
- Where and when the item was found, e.g. mobile phone seized from X on arrest on 31/07/23.
- Who the item is attributed to.

Naming conventions

In large or more complex cases, it may also help if advising on disclosure at an early stage, to set out in advance what naming conventions should be used in drafting the descriptions of items on the MG6C. For example, there should be consistency in how dates are recorded, e.g. 31/07/2023 or 31.7.23. Telephone numbers may be sensitive and, again, a consistent convention of, say, redacting all but the last four digits can be agreed.

Disclosure Management Documents

The purpose of a Disclosure Management Document ('DMD') is for the prosecution to set out in a transparent way how disclosure has been managed in the case to-date as well as explaining the continuing and future scope of the disclosure exercise. When prosecuting, ask the CPS at an early stage for a copy of the DMD or at least a draft version, so you can see the approach that has been taken. When the DMD has been prepared, ensure that it has been uploaded to section UND1 of the Digital Case System so the defence and the court have access to it.

The DMD should make clear to the defence and to the court what the prosecution are doing, and what they do not intend to do. It should identify what has been considered by the Disclosure Officer and the Prosecutor to be the reasonable lines of enquiry in the case together with a comprehensive summary, where appropriate, as to how all seized electronic devices and third party material has been dealt with.

Paragraphs 93 to 99 of the Attorney General's Guidelines on Disclosure (2022) provide the following guidance in relation to Disclosure Management Documents,

> *"93. A disclosure management document (DMD) outlines the strategy and approach taken in relation to disclosure and should be served to the defence and the court at an early stage. DMDs will require careful preparation and presentation which is tailored to the individual case.*

The investigator should provide information for use in the DMD and the prosecutor should prepare it.

94. A DMD is a living document which should be amended in light of developments in the case and kept up to date as the case progresses. DMDs are intended to assist the court in case management and will also enable the defence to engage from an early stage with the prosecution's proposed approach to disclosure.

95. DMDs may set out:

a. Where prosecutors and investigators operate in an integrated office, an explanation as to how the disclosure responsibilities have been managed.

b. A brief summary of the prosecution case and a statement outlining how the prosecutor's general approach will comply with the CPIA 1996 regime and these guidelines.

c. The prosecutor's understanding of the defence case, including information revealed during interview. The prosecutor may wish to explain their understanding of what is in dispute and what is not in dispute, the lines of inquiry that have been pursued in light of these issues, and specific disclosure decisions that have been taken.

d. An outline of the prosecution's general approach to disclosure, which may include detail relating to:

> *i. The lines of inquiry pursued, particularly those which may assist the defence.*
>
> *ii. The timescales for disclosure and, where relevant, how the review of unused material has been prioritised.*

iii. The method and extent of examination of digital material, in accordance with Annex A to these guidelines.

iv. Any potential video footage.

v. Any linked investigations, including an explanation of the nexus between investigations and may memoranda of understanding and disclosure agreements between investigators.

vi. Any third party material, including the steps taken to obtain the material.

vii. Any international material, including the steps taken to obtain the material.

viii. Credibility of prosecution witnesses (including professional witnesses).

96. In cases heard in the magistrates' court and the youth court, prosecutors should always consider whether or not a disclosure management document (DMD) would be beneficial. DMDs are most likely to be beneficial in cases with the following features:

a. Substantial or complex third party material;

b. Digital material in which parameters of search, examination or analysis have been set;

c. Cases involving international enquiries;

d. Cases where there are linked operations;

e. No-recent offending;

f. Cases involving material held or sought by the investigation that is susceptible to a claim of legal professional privilege.

97. DMDs should be prepared in all Crown Court cases.

98. In order for the prosecutor to complete a DMD at an early stage, the investigator should, at the point of or prior to charge, provide written details as to the lines of inquiry that have been pursued.

99. Where a DMD has been prepared, it should be served at the same time as initial disclosure."

Annex C of the Attorney General's Guidelines on Disclosure (2022) provides the following suggested DMD template:

"Template "Disclosure Management Document"

This Disclosure Management Document sets out the approach of the prosecution to relevant non-sensitive material in this case. Unless otherwise indicated, all the material on the non-sensitive schedule has been inspected by the disclosure officer.

R v [Name]

Prosecutor:

Disclosure officer:

Prosecution counsel instructed:

1. Reasonable lines of inquiry

The rationale for the identification and scheduling of relevant material is based upon the reasonable lines of inquiry that were conducted within this investigation. The Disclosure Officer's understanding of the defence case is as follows;

- *[What explanation has been offered by the accused, whether in formal interview, defence statement or otherwise. How has this been followed up? This should be set out.]*

- *[What are the identified/likely issues in the case e.g. identification, alibi, factual dispute, no intention etc]*

- *[Insert summary of reasonable lines of enquiry pursued, particularly those that point away from the suspect, or which may assist the defence]*

- *The time frame selected is considered to be a reasonable line of inquiry, and represents [e.g. the date that the victim first met the suspect to a month after the suspect's arrest]*

2. Electronic material

This section should cover the following issues.

- *What mobile telephones/communication devices/computers were seized during the investigation (from all suspects, complainants, witnesses).*

- *Identify the items with reference to the schedule of materials – i.e. telephone, download*

- *Have the devices been downloaded? If not, why not. If so, what type of download?*

- *Set out the method of examination of each download – were key words deployed, was the entire download inspected, were date parameters employed?*

- *What social media accounts of suspect/complaint/witness have been considered a reasonable line of enquiry.*

- *Were any phones from the complainant or suspect not seized? If not, why not?*

- *Set out the method by which the defence will be given disclosure of material that satisfies the disclosure test explaining, if relevant, why the whole item is not being provided.*

- *What CCTV/multi-media evidence has been seized and how it has been examined?*

A suggested presentation and wording of the information is set out below:

Exhibit ref	***Description***	***Enquiry undertaken***	***Result***
AB/1	*I-phone seized from defendant*	*This telephone has been downloaded using the XRY software. This has resulted in 40,000 pages of data which includes telephone calls to and from the suspect, contact list, text messages, WhatsApp messages and internet search history. No further data has been downloaded from the phone.* *The internet search history does not appear to be relevant to the issues in the case and has not been reviewed.* *The contact list has been reviewed to identify whether the complainant is a contact, no further checks have been made.* *The telephone call list has been reviewed for any contact between the suspect and complainant between dates x and y. All identified contact has been produced as exhibit AB/2.* *Text messages and WhatsApp messages have been searched using the following keywords [A, B, C, D] all responsive messages which correspond with the keywords have been disclosed.* *No further checks have been conducted upon the phone.*	*Relevant evidential material has been served.* *Material which has been identified through keyword searching has been collated and scheduled. The defence are invited to identify any further keywords which might represent a reasonable line of enquiry. If further interrogation of the telephone is considered to be necessary the defence are invited to identify what enquiries should be undertaken and identify the relevance of such enquiries to the issues in this case.*

3. Third Party Material

The prosecution believe that the following third parties have relevant non-sensitive material that might satisfy the disclosure test if it were in the possession of the prosecution (e.g. Medical and dental records, Records held by other agencies, Records/material held by Social Services or local authority):

The reason for this belief is ...
The type of relevant material is...
The following steps have been taken to obtain this material:

The defence have a critical role in ensuring that the prosecution is directed to material that meets the disclosure test. Any representations by the defence on the contents of this document, including identifying issues in the case and why material meets the test for disclosure should be received by [insert date/ timescale]."

Signed: *Dated:"*

Providing the defence and the court with a Disclosure Management Document in advance of the PTPH, allows for early scrutiny of the approach to disclosure. Any challenges to that approach can then be aired at an early stage, allowing for further appropriate directions to be made and any identified deficiency in the process to be remedied well before the trial.

PTPH form

The Plea & Trial Preparation Hearing form specifically addresses Disclosure Management Documents. Orders that may be made at the PTPH include service of an updated or initial DMD (to address issues raised by the defence on the PTPH form) by the Stage 1 date, defence response by the Stage 2 date and any further updated DMD to be served by the Stage 3 date.

Sensitive material

In all cases, care should be taken to review the material that is scheduled on the MG6D, to see if as much of it as possible can be moved onto the MG6C. In other words, examine whether what is on the MG6D is really sensitive material. One approach that should be adopted is, where possible, to move items from the MG6D to the MG6C, but to mark it "sensitive can be edited" where only a discreet part of the document is sensitive. If, in due course, that document is disclosed, it can be disclosed in a redacted format.

Continuity of Disclosure Officers

In larger and more complex cases, particularly those that have involved long investigations, there can be a danger that there is a break in the continuity of key personnel in the disclosure team. It is important, therefore, to ensure that if a disclosure officer, in particular the lead disclosure officer, leaves the disclosure team before the trial, for example due to retirement or re-deployment, that there is an adequate handover to those taking over.

Instructing Disclosure Counsel

It may be helpful to instruct a Disclosure Counsel in cases where there is a large volume of unused material or where there are particular disclosure issues such as the need to review sensitive material. The precise role of a Disclosure Counsel may vary from case to case. A Disclosure Counsel does not replace the functions of the disclosure officer or the reviewing lawyer. However, a Disclosure Counsel can quality control the disclosure process, advise on best practice, assist in reviewing unused material and add a further, independent review layer to help ensure that all material that passes the disclosure test is disclosed.

Statistics

In larger and more complex cases it is prudent to ask the disclosure officer to provide an estimate of the number of items of unused material that have been reviewed and the number that are yet to be assessed for disclosure. This information should be supplied to trial counsel who can then provide the court and defence with an accurate idea of how far the disclosure process has left to go at critical hearings such as the PTPH. This may be relevant not only to when the prosecution are ordered to complete initial disclosure by but also when fixing the trial date. There is no point in setting the case down for trial on a date that will be too soon for the disclosure exercise to be completed by. A court may be willing to provide a more generous timeframe if there is a clear indication of the scale of the disclosure exercise.

DEFENCE PERSPECTIVE

The early identification of issues by the defence will increase the chances of timely and effective disclosure by the prosecution. A court will also be more sympathetic to defence representations in relation to an issue that is raised early rather than at the last minute or during the trial. The following checklist, which duplicates many of the points set out in the prosecution checklist above, may be of assistance to those acting for the defence.

DEFENCE CHECKLIST

- What are the deadlines for initial disclosure, service of the defence statement, prosecution response to the defence statement, and any timetable relating to disclosure requests / section 8 applications and responses?
- Has an initial disclosure (section 3) letter been received?
- Confirm with the prosecution what the date of the last MG6C is and what item number that MG6C goes up to.
- Check whether there are any gaps in the MG6Cs that have been provided by the prosecution.
- Confirm with the prosecution what further unused material, if any, is still to be reviewed, and when that exercise will be completed by.
- Are the descriptions on the MG6C clear and informative? If not, ask for clarification.
- Are all the MG6Cs signed and dated by the disclosure officer and reviewing lawyer?
- Have all entries been endorsed, for example CND or D?
- Have all the items marked as disclosable actually been disclosed?
- Have the MG6Cs been uploaded to the Digital Case System?
- Have the contents of the defence statement been verified by the client and signed and dated before service?

- Has the defence statement been uploaded to the Digital Case System?

- Does the defence statement identify the real issues in the case? If not, is it worth providing a supplementary defence statement, clarifying the defence on any particular issues?

- Has a defence witness notice been served?

- Please see **Chapter Four** for further analysis of the content of defence statements and witness notices.

- Ask the prosecutor to confirm that the disclosure officer has seen a copy of the defence statement and when.

- Has there been a written response to the defence statement?

- Is the response adequate? If not, raise this in correspondence with the prosecution.

- Have appropriate disclosure requests been made in writing?

- Is it necessary to make a written section 8 application?

- Is it necessary to list the case in order to make a section 8 application to the court?

- Please see **Chapter Five** for examples of disclosure requests and the section 8 application process.

- For cases involving Digital Material, please refer to the points raised in **Chapter Seven**.

- For cases involving expert witnesses, please refer to the checklist we have set out in **Chapter Eight**.

- Ask the prosecution to confirm whether there are any outstanding enquiries, linked investigations and what third party material there is.

- Has consideration been given to the defence conducting its own enquiries, for example with third parties?

- Ask the prosecution whether there is any international material, whether there are any ongoing international enquiries, when any such enquiries are expected to be completed by and when the decision was taken to pursue those enquiries?

- Has the Disclosure Management Document (DMD) been uploaded to the Digital Case System?

- Does the Disclosure Management Document identify, (a) what the issues in the case are, and (b) set out the reasonable lines of enquiry that have been pursued? If not, raise this with the prosecution in writing and, if necessary, promptly bring any concerns to the court's attention. There are also specific boxes on the PTPH form, at pages 3 and 9, which provide the defence with an opportunity to set out why they consider the DMD to be inadequate and to suggest what other lines of enquiry should be pursued.

- Seek confirmation from prosecution counsel that they themselves are satisfied that the prosecution have discharged all of their disclosure obligations.

- Even if disclosure has been provided, consider if it has been provided in sufficient time to allow the material to be considered with the client. If not, and if necessary, ask the court for time to review the material.

- If there are concerns about the adequacy of the disclosure exercise, raise this in writing with the prosecution and court and, if necessary, consider making an application to exclude evidence under section 78 of PACE, prompt the prosecution to make an application to adjourn in order to remedy any disclosure failings or even, as a last resort, consider making an application to stay proceedings. These options are considered further in **Chapter Twelve.**

Potential problems to look out for

In addition to the points raised above we set out below some specific errors to look out for:

- Unused material not scheduled.
- Poor description of items on the MG6C.
- Material that passes the disclosure test not disclosed.
- Reasonable lines of enquiry not pursued.
- Disclosure enquiries remaining outstanding at date of trial.
- Inadequate defence statements.
- Inadequate responses to defence statements.
- Failure to review unused material.
- Failure to review material previously deemed 'non-relevant'.
- Electronic devices such as mobile phones and laptops not effectively reviewed.

- Failure of the defence to engage in the disclosure process until shortly before or during the trial.

- Inadequate training provided to those who are tasked with reviewing unused material.

- Poor communication between officers who are tasked with reviewing unused material and the investigation team who prepare the evidence for trial.

- Lack of early intervention by the trial judge to manage the disclosure process.

CHAPTER TWELVE

TACKLING DISCLOSURE PROBLEMS

In the last chapter we looked at steps to take to avoid any errors in the disclosure process from arising. In this chapter, we consider the best way to tackle the most common types of disclosure problems if they do in fact present themselves. Again, we take a look at the response that can be taken from both the prosecution and defence perspectives.

PROSECUTION PERSPECTIVE

The following are examples of disclosure issues that may arise:

- It becomes clear that a document that should have been disclosed was not disclosed but instead was either not even on an MG6C or, if it was, was poorly described or marked 'Clearly Not Disclosable'. This prompts the defence to ask if the prosecution have made such a mistake in relation to this item, what other mistakes have been made?

- It is discovered that an item of electronic media, such as a computer hard drive, has not been reviewed for disclosure or not been reviewed properly.

- There is still material that needs to be reviewed and there is a risk that the disclosure review will not be completed in time to comply with the timetable set by the court.

What are the practical ways forward for the prosecution when faced with such disclosure problems?

- Review the disclosure process.
- Provide further disclosure that passes the disclosure test.
- Seek an adjournment or an extension of time to find out why a disclosure failing has arisen and to remedy the problem by ensuring that all material that passes the disclosure test has been disclosed.
- Ensure that adequate resources are deployed in the further review of disclosure.
- Consider whether it would be helpful to provide a further Disclosure Management Document, setting out what went wrong and how any problems have now been remedied.

If there has been a breakdown in the disclosure process, consideration should be given to immediately holding an urgent conference between Counsel, the OIC, the disclosure officer, and the reviewing lawyer.

Depending on the particular issue, it will be necessary to ensure as a minimum that that all material has been properly scheduled on an MG6C, that all the items on the MG6C have been correctly categorised (i.e. marked whether they are disclosable or not) and that there are no outstanding disclosure requests that have not been properly responded to. It will also be helpful to review the Disclosure Record Sheet to examine the chronology of the disclosure process and what has gone wrong.

A realistic assessment of the further work that needs to be conducted must take place in order to inform the decision as to whether to seek and adjournment, and if so for what period of time.

It will be important to identify whether the disclosure failing is as a result of a one-off human error or whether there is a more fundamental problem with the disclosure process as a whole.

It may be helpful to prepare a bundle of key documents such as Disclosure Management Documents, together with any disclosure requests and responses. A further Disclosure Management Document may also be required to bring the defence and court completely up to date with the disclosure process.

DEFENCE PERSPECTIVE

The following are some of the options available to the defence when confronted with a disclosure failing:

- Renew any previously denied section 8 applications.
- Request that the prosecution review the adequacy of their disclosure process, including whether they need to review the accuracy of the descriptions of items of unused material on the MG6C.
- Apply to exclude evidence pursuant to section 78 of PACE.
- Ask for the prosecution to confirm whether or not they have complied with their disclosure obligations.
- Apply, or prompt the prosecution to apply, to adjourn the case until such time as the prosecution have complied with their disclosure obligations.
- Apply to stay the proceedings as an abuse of process.

Section 78 applications

Section 78(1) of the *Police and Criminal Evidence Act* 1984 provides that,

> *"In any proceedings the court may refuse to allow evidence on which the prosecution proposes to rely to be given if it appears to the court that, having regard to all the circumstances, including the circumstances in which the evidence was obtained, the admission of the evidence would have such an adverse effect on the fairness of the proceedings that the court ought not to admit it."*

One example that may arise is if the prosecution makes late disclosure, for example the existence of a witness, which then leaves the defence with inadequate time to carry out any consequential investigations themselves, such as seeking a statement from the said witness. The defence could then argue that, pursuant to section 78 of PACE, the evidence relating to the issue covered by that witness should be excluded.

Application for an adjournment

If the prosecution have disclosed material late, it may be worth considering asking for time or to seek an adjournment, to ensure that the defence team are on top of the new material. Consideration, for example, may need to be given to deploying the lately disclosed material in cross-examination.

Time will also often be needed to put disclosed material into a format that can be presented to the jury, such as a defence jury bundle. Submissions could be made that the defence should not be placed under pressure of time to consider material that should have been disclosed some time ago.

On the other hand, if the prosecution are at fault and have still not properly complied with their disclosure obligations, it is the prosecution not the defence who should be applying to adjourn the case to allow any outstanding disclosure issues to be remedied.

Prosecution offering no evidence

Where the court refuses a prosecution application to adjourn to fix any shortcomings in the disclosure process, the defence should invite the prosecution to offer no evidence.

In *DPP v Petrie* [2015] EWHC 48 (Admin), Lord Justice Gross stated at paragraph 39,

> *"The manner in which this case proceeded prompts a number of reflections:...*
>
> *In some cases, a wholesale failure on the part of the prosecution to comply with its disclosure obligations may require the prosecution to offer no evidence, in accordance with the professional code for prosecutors and the guidance set out in the CPS/ACPO Disclosure Manual: see, Magistrates' Court Disclosure Review, 2014, by HHJ Kinch QC and The Chief Magistrate, at para. 148. That is not this case but the possibility of such an outcome serves to illuminate that only rarely will recourse to an abuse of process argument be necessary or appropriate."*

Paragraph 148 of the Magistrates' Court Disclosure Review 2014, referred to in *Petrie*, states,

> *"If the application for an adjournment is refused, the consequence must be that the prosecution should offer no evidence... It would be against the professional code of conduct for prosecutors to proceed to trial having not complied with their statutory disclosure obligations. Generally, an abuse of process argument is neither necessary nor appropriate."*

Application to stay proceedings as an abuse of process

It is important to properly consider the impact of a disclosure failure. Often, it will be capable of remedy, for example by disclosing a document that should have been disclosed at an earlier stage of proceedings. However, occasionally, where the disclosure failure reveals problems with the integrity, adequacy or competence of the investigation and/or prosecution, it may be appropriate for the proceedings to be stayed as an abuse of process.

There are two main categories of abuse of process argument:

- Submitting that the defendant cannot receive a fair trial.
- Submitting that it would be unfair to try the defendant.

As was stated by the Court of Appeal in *Crawley* [2014] EWCA Crim 1028, at paragraph 17,

> *"As is clear from decisions such as Attorney General's Reference (No 2 of 2001) [2004] 2 AC 72, there are two categories of case in which the court has the power to stay proceedings for abuse of process. These are, first, where the court concludes that the accused can no longer receive a fair hearing; and, second, where it would otherwise be unfair to try the accused or, put another way, where a stay is necessary to protect the integrity of the criminal justice system. The first limb focuses on the trial process and where the court concludes that the accused would not receive a fair hearing it will stay the proceedings; no balancing exercise is required. The second limb concerns the integrity of the criminal justice system and applies where the Court considers that the accused should not be standing trial at all, irrespective of the potential fairness of the trial itself."*

An example of a limb one argument would be where there was a fundamental problem with the way in which the prosecution had sought to discharge their disclosure obligations, for example not properly reviewing the digital material.

An example of a limb two argument would be where there was evidence that an officer had acted in bad faith by withholding or even destroying disclosable material.

In *R v Salt* [2015] 1 WLR 4905, the defendants were charged with rape, false imprisonment and assault by penetration. The trial judge allowed the defendant's application that the proceedings be stayed as an abuse of process on the basis that the prosecution's failure to make proper disclosure of unused material was so fundamental that, although a future trial could be held fairly, the court ought to mark its condemnation by allowing a stay.

The Court of Appeal in *Salt* allowed the prosecution's appeal, holding that where the court was considering making a ruling that would bring proceedings to an end, either by refusing to admit evidence or ordering a stay of proceedings, the court should approach its decision by determining whether it was in the interests of justice for proceedings to continue, balancing the public interest in ensuring that those charged with serious offences should be tried and the rights of complainants to have their allegations determined at trial against the need to ensure the integrity of the criminal justice system and the fairness of any future trial.

The Court of Appeal in *Salt* then identified the following considerations that were material in that case:

- the gravity of the charges;
- the denial of justice to the complainants;
- the necessity for proper attention to be paid to disclosure;
- the nature and materiality of the prosecution's failures;
- the waste of court resources and the effect on the jury; and
- the availability of other sanctions, including a wasted costs order.

On the facts of *Salt*, the Court of Appeal ultimately found that as the material that had not been disclosed was restricted to telephone records and was only relevant to the issue of credibility, it would not be in the interests of justice to stay proceedings.

Before an abuse of process argument is considered, it may be necessary to first call evidence, for example the disclosure officer, on a *voir dire* to determine the precise basis for the application to stay.

When making an application to stay a case, reference should also be made to the procedural requirements of CrimPR 3.28:

> ***"Application to stay case for abuse of process***
>
> ***3.28.***—*(1) This rule applies where a defendant wants the Crown Court to stay the case on the grounds that the proceedings are an abuse of the court, or otherwise unfair.*
>
> *(2) Such a defendant must—*
>
> *(a) apply in writing—*
>
> *(i) as soon as practicable after becoming aware of the grounds for doing so,*
>
> *(ii) at a pre-trial hearing, unless the grounds for the application do not arise until trial, and*
>
> *(iii) in any event, before the defendant pleads guilty or the jury (if there is one) retires to consider its verdict at trial;*
>
> *(b) serve the application on—*
>
> *(i) the court officer, and*
>
> *(ii) each other party; and*

(c) in the application—

(i) explain the grounds on which it is made,

(ii) include, attach or identify all supporting material,

(iii) specify relevant events, dates and propositions of law, and

(iv) identify any witness the applicant wants to call to give evidence in person.

(3) A party who wants to make representations in response to the application must serve the representations on—

(a) the court officer; and

(b) each other party,

not more than 10 business days after service of the application.

Abuse of process applications in the magistrates' court

In magistrates' court proceedings, whilst an application to stay proceedings on the basis that the defendant cannot receive a fair trial can properly be made in appropriate cases; where the submission is on the ground that it would be unfair to try the defendant, the latter application should be made to the High Court.

Lord Griffiths in the House of Lords decision in *Horseferry Road Magistrates Court, ex parte Bennett* [1994] 1 AC 42 at 64, stated,

> *"I would accordingly affirm the power of the magistrates, whether sitting as committing justices or exercising their summary jurisdiction, to exercise control over their proceedings through an abuse of process jurisdiction. However, in the case of magistrates this power should be strictly confined to matters directly affecting the fairness of the trial of the particular accused with whom they are dealing, such as delay or*

unfair manipulation of court procedures. Although it may be convenient to label the wider supervisory jurisdiction with which we are concerned in this appeal under the head of abuse of process, it is in fact a horse of a very different colour from the narrower issues that arise when considering domestic criminal trial procedures. I adhere to the view I expressed in Reg. v. Guildford Magistrates' Court, Ex parte Healy [1983] 1 W.L.R. 108 that this wider responsibility for upholding the rule of law must be that of the High Court and that if a serious question arises as to the deliberate abuse of extradition procedures a magistrate should allow an adjournment so that an application can be made to the Divisional Court which I regard as the proper forum in which such a decision should be taken."

Challenging applications to extend the custody time limit

Where an adjournment is possible and a client is in custody, consider challenging an extension of the custody time limit, on the grounds that the prosecution have not acted with, *"all due diligence and expedition"* and/or that there is no, *"good and sufficient cause"* to extend an unconvicted defendant's pre-trial detention.

Section 22(3) of the *Prosecution of Offences Act* 1985, sets out the criteria to be met when making an application to extend the custody time limit.

"(3) The appropriate court may, at any time before the expiry of a time limit imposed by the regulations, extend, or further extend, that limit; but the court shall not do so unless it is satisfied—

(a) that the need for the extension is due to—

(i) the illness or absence of the accused, a necessary witness, a judge or a magistrate;

(ii) a postponement which is occasioned by the ordering by the court of separate trials in the case of two or more accused or two or more offences; or

(iii) some other good and sufficient cause; and

(b) that the prosecution has acted with all due diligence and expedition."

R (Hughes) v Woolwich Crown Court [2006] EWHC 2191, was a judicial review of a Crown Court judge's decision to refuse a defence submission that the custody time limit should not be extended. The Divisional Court quashed the judge's decision, making the following observations:

"12. [The Trial Judge] took the view, and correctly took the view, that the defence had failed in its duty to serve a defence statement in time. He approached the matter on the basis that that was, as it were, the trigger date for the prosecution to obtain the material. He considered to have got as far as they had by 4th August – because it transpired that the material was available by the beginning of the following week – showed that they had applied themselves diligently.

13. [Defence Counsel] makes the point that it was wrong to treat that as the trigger date, because there was knowledge by the prosecution at a much earlier stage that these records might be material. The prosecution has a duty, as is well known, to investigate all material matters, whether or not they might serve to support the prosecution case. Even if one takes the view that it was not reasonable to expect them to appreciate the possible significance of these records when they received the statement from the defendant, it is clear that by April 2006, when counsel advised, they were aware of the significance and, as counsel correctly indicated, it was necessary to see whether those records did or did not support the account given by the defendant. It seems to me that they were clearly of possible materiality, either as supporting the prosecution case, if they showed that the defendant had not been telling the truth when he asserted that there had been virtually daily communication, or as possibly supporting the defence case if they did show that. Accordingly, on either account they might be material. But certainly on the basis, as prosecuting counsel himself recognised, that they might support the defence contentions.

> *14. However, as I say, due I am told to a misunderstanding although it is difficult to follow quite why the clear advice should have been misunderstood, the records were not obtained. There then comes the letter of 23rd June, which explicitly refers to the records and makes it clear that the defence wanted them and that if the prosecution did not have them, the defence should be notified and would if necessary make the appropriate application to the court. Nothing was done by the prosecuting authorities in answer to that letter. Then comes the defence statement. It seems to me that the learned judge ought at the very least to have had regard to the previous letter of 23rd June, because that put the matter clearly. It is not necessary to wait for a formal defence statement for the prosecution to take the necessary steps to ensure that the trial takes place within the proper time. True it is that 23rd June was somewhat late in the day, with only a month before the date of the fixture. But as it seems to me there was no conceivable excuse for the failure to act, and indeed the failure to reply to the letter of 23rd June. That is a relevant factor which the learned judge ought to have taken into account. It seems to me too that he ought to have had regard to the fact that prosecuting counsel advised, back in April, of the materiality or the possible materiality of these records."*

This case is a reminder that disclosure issues can also properly be raised in correspondence, even before the service of a defence statement.

We set out below a series of case studies. Whilst the facts are not identical to actual cases, they nevertheless give examples of how some of the issues we have raised in this book may arise in practice.

Case study 1: Defence taken by surprise

The defence advocate attends the magistrates' court to defend her client who is charged with criminal damage of a car window. The allegation is that the defendant threw a brick, twice, at a car window until it smashed. The defence is that the defendant saw a dog in distress in the car on a hot summer's day and believed that the owner would have consented to him breaking the window to save the dog. Shortly before the bench enter court, the prosecution advocate asks the defence advocate whether she has seen the officer's notebook. She hands the defence advocate a police officer's notebook in which the officer recorded an account by a witness who had described seeing the defendant, "walk away" from the scene after he had smashed the car window. The defence argue that this notebook entry should have been disclosed and seek an adjournment to see if the witness can be identified with a view to being a potential defence witness. The bench refuse the application to adjourn but grant the defence advocate's second application, which is for the evidence of one of the prosecution's witnesses that they saw the defendant, "running" away from the scene to be ruled inadmissible pursuant to section 78 of PACE given the late disclosure by the prosecution.

Case study 2: Prosecution taken by surprise

A defendant is charged with GBH. The defence statement claims that it is a case of mistaken identity. On the day of trial, the defence serve a revised defence statement, in which the defendant now admits presence at the scene and being involved in the fight but claims to have acted in self-defence. The prosecution cross-examine the defendant on the fact that he had denied even being present at the scene in his defence statement and has now come up with a new defence at trial. The defendant asserts that he never read the original defence statement. The prosecution then make an application to adduce the original defence statement in evidence before the jury on the basis that it provided a false account of being elsewhere at the time of the assault. The trial-judge allows the application pursuant to section 6E of the CPIA 1996. After the end of the defendant's evidence, the defence take instructions but decide not to waive privilege by calling the solicitor who drafted the original defence statement. The judge, after hearing submissions from the prosecution and defence, directs the jury that they can draw an adverse inference from the defendant's failure to set out his defence in his original defence statement.

Case study 3: OIC has not had sight of the defence statement

The defendant is charged with burglary. On the morning of trial, it becomes clear that the Officer in the Case has not been provided with a copy of the defence statement. The defence statement, which had been served in time, and a number of months before the trial, sets out the defence that at the time of the burglary the defendant was at a hostel in another part of the country. The defence statement also provides contact details for the manager of the hostel. The defence, in correspondence, had also referred the prosecution to the defendant's defence and details of the manager, adding that the manager refused to engage with the defence. The defence solicitors also pointed out that they believed that the hostel has CCTV, which would show the defendant in the hostel at the time of the burglary.

The OIC states that he needs time to carry out further investigations in light of the defence statement. The prosecution witnesses have all attended court and are ready to give their evidence. Defence counsel submits that the trial cannot proceed until the prosecution have discharged their disclosure obligations. The prosecution agree and apply to adjourn the trial in order to make the necessary enquiries with the hostel manager referred to in the defence statement.

Prosecution counsel also submits that it is not entirely the fault of the prosecution, as the defence could themselves have sought a witness summons to compel the hostel manager to produce any relevant CCTV. The prosecution's application to adjourn is, however, refused. The prosecution then offer no evidence after concluding that they cannot properly continue with the trial given that they have not properly discharged their disclosure obligations.

Case study 4: Late disclosure

The defendant is in his 50s and of good character, having previously worked as a carer for old people. The allegation is that he stole nearly £10,000 from a vulnerable old man by using his bank card and pin number over a period of two years. The issue was raised by the complainant's daughter. She reported the matter to the police saying that the money had gone missing. By then the complainant was not fit enough to provide evidence on the subject.

When the defendant was arrested, he immediately denied the allegation and set out in full an account that the old man had asked him to get the money for shopping and the excess balance was to be left in a drawer in the bedside table so that he could assist a friend of his who had fallen on hard times.

The defence repeatedly requested access to social services files and reports from other carers during the relevant time. None were provided, despite the case taking a long time to be listed for trial.

On the Friday before trial, the police and CPS produced the file that the defence had been asking for. Defence counsel spent the weekend reading the files and they revealed a picture which wholly supported the defendant's account: the elderly man telling carers at the time that he had asked the defendant to obtain money for him in the approximate sums alleged so that he could assist an old friend of his who had fallen on hard times. This was confirmed by a number of independent carers and social service supervisors who queried the old man's generosity and were told that he knew perfectly well what he was doing and he intended to carry on doing it. As a result of this late disclosure, the prosecution offered no evidence on the first day of trial.

Case study 5: Inadequate keyword searches

The defendant faces a number of counts of fraud and false accounting. In relation to the fraud counts, the defendant in his defence statement denied dishonesty and sought disclosure of any emails from satisfied customers that indicated that the defendant had been operating a legitimate business. At trial it becomes clear that there was no consistent approach or proper records kept of what keywords were used on which device. Attempts are made by the prosecution during the trial itself to try to remedy the problem by running fresh searches relevant to the fraud counts, across emails that were contained on a number of devices. However, there is insufficient time for this work to be carried out in a proper manner. The court refuse the prosecution application for a longer adjournment. The defence invite the prosecution to confirm whether, in the circumstances, they can say that they have discharged their disclosure obligations in relation to the fraud counts. The prosecution end up offering no evidence on the fraud counts and the trial proceeds on a much more limited basis on the false accounting counts alone.

Case study 6: Section 8 application

The defendant is charged with wounding with intent. The defendant claims in his defence statement that it was in fact a prosecution eye-witness who was the person who committed the stabbing and that he intervened, grabbing the kitchen knife in order to try to protect the victim from further attack. The defence make repeated requests in correspondence for the prosecution to disclose any material which supports their case that it was the prosecution witness who carried out the attack. The prosecution disclose the witness's PNC printout, which includes previous convictions for violence and possession of an offensive weapon.

The defence serve a bad character notice and also a section 8 application. The section 8 application makes reference to the defence statement and the bad character application to justify why disclosure of material, such as case summaries and case papers in relation to the prosecution witness's previous convictions for violence and possession of an offensive weapon, should be disclosed.

The section 8 application is granted. The prosecution subsequently disclose details of the facts behind the relevant previous convictions, some of which included use of a knife. This helps the defence's bad character application to succeed and allows them to deploy the details from the previous cases in cross-examination of the prosecution witness.

Case study 7: CCTV is not on the MG6C

The defendant is charged with being drunk and disorderly in a public place. The MG6C does not contain CCTV from the council that would have covered the scene. The defence serve a defence statement and request the CCTV, explaining that it would show that the defendant did not display any signs of drunkenness at all.

The prosecution inform the defence that the CCTV footage will be brought to court. However, on the day of trial, the prosecutor does not have the CCTV. He confirms it exists but that it has not been reviewed and that the OIC has stated that it is in a format that cannot be viewed on laptops without special software.

Defence counsel explains to the magistrates that the CCTV should have been on the unused schedule and that the prosecutor's admission that it has not been reviewed means that the prosecution have not complied with their disclosure obligations and so cannot proceed with the case.

The prosecutor then asks defence counsel if she is making an application to adjourn. Defence counsel replies that it should be the prosecution's application, not the defence's, and that the defence opposed an adjournment. The prosecution point out that this is in fact the first time the case had been listed for trial and that it is in the interests of justice to grant the adjournment in order to review the CCTV material.

The prosecution application is refused, the court noting that not only had the CCTV not been brought to court, but that it should have been scheduled on the MG6C. The prosecution ultimately offer no evidence, being unable to comply with their disclosure obligations.

CHAPTER THIRTEEN

REMUNERATION

In this chapter we consider the guidance in relation to making a claim for considering unused material. In most cases, payment for advocates viewing up to three hours of unused material is covered by the fixed fee with any reasonable time spent considering unused material over and above the three hours, paid at an hourly rate on production of detailed work logs.

Defence fees

The latest version of the Crown Court Fee Guidance was issued in April 2023.

Paragraph 2.16A of the Guidance states:

> ***"2.16A Fees for consideration of unused material***
>
> *1. Payment for considering unused material may be claimed in respect of any case on indictment in the Crown Court (other than a guilty plea) with a representation order dated on or after 17 September 2020. A fixed fee is payable for viewing 0-3 hours of material. Material considered which is in excess of 3 hours is payable at the hourly rates specified and may be claimed in addition to the fixed fee for the first 3 hours. Paragraph 17A, Schedule 1 of the Remuneration Regulations sets out the circumstances where the consideration of unused material may be claimed.*
>
> *2. Consideration of unused material of 3 hours or less should be claimed as a fixed fee on CCD. If the time for considering unused material is in excess of 3 hours a claim must be made using form AU1 together with a supporting work log (for claims in excess of 10 hours).*

The schedule of unused material and Disclosure Management Document (DMD) or other documentation evidencing disclosure of unused material must also be provided with your claim.

3. The appropriate officer must take into account:

(a) the reasonableness of the hours claimed in respect of the case taken as a whole; and

(b) the reasonableness of the hours claimed in respect of the consideration of the unused material.

The larger the claim the more detailed justification would be expected…"

Appendix D, paragraph 3(a), confirms that Pages of Prosecution Evidence (PPE) do not include Unused Material.

Note Appendix D, paragraph 22:

"22. Whether electronically served material should be included within the PPE depends upon its substance, relevance, importance and context. The fact that material was served and may have contained relevant data or data supportive of the Defendant's case is not, by itself, sufficient basis for inclusion within the PPE. A defence representative is under a duty to review all evidence irrespective of relevance or whether it is served as used evidence or disclosed as unused material."

Appendix D paragraphs 56-68 provide guidance in relation to claiming for unused material:

"Unused Material

56. The Criminal Procedure and Investigations Act 1986 (CPIA) requires prosecutors to disclose to the defence material which has not previously been disclosed to the accused and which might reasonably be considered capable of undermining the case for the prosecution against the accused or of assisting the case for the accused. Such material falls within the category of unused material.

57. Unused material is not payable for cases with a representation order dated before 17 September 2020. For cases with a representation order on or after 17 September 2020, payment for unused material is made separately (see Appendix E), and it is not included within the PPE proxy.

58. Advance disclosure does not count towards PPE. This is because such evidence is often duplicated in the committal or first prosecution bundle.

59. However, in circumstances where the case concludes before the prosecution documents are served, and it does not fall within paragraph 22 of Schedule 1 of the Remuneration Regulations (i.e., is not discontinued or dismissed), and the PPE count is relevant, the correct number of pages of PPE is the material served on the court for the purposes of enabling the Judge to deal with the case, which is usually similar to the advance disclosure bundle.

60. In the majority of cases, it should be clear whether material has been served as used prosecution evidence (as it will be included in an NAE) or disclosed as unused material. However, in Lord Chancellor v Edward Hayes [2017] EWHC 138 (QB), the High Court held that defence practitioners should not be penalised for lack of formal service. Therefore, where evidence was served without an NAE, but was clearly integral to the prosecution case it should be treated as PPE.

61. Where there is an issue regarding the status of certain material, the determining officer should have regard to the principles set out in paragraph 50 of Lord Chancellor v SVS Solicitors (2017) EWHC 1045 (QB). This decision re-affirmed that lack of formal service should not necessarily preclude evidence from being included within the PPE count, and emphasised the desirability of all parties reaching an agreement about the status of particular material prior to billing, either by negotiation or, exceptionally, by ruling of the trial judge.

62. It should only be in exceptional circumstances that a claim is submitted to the LAA for payment where issues regarding the status of the material have not been resolved. Any evidence of attempts to resolve the status of the material between the parties including applications to the trial judge should be drawn to the determining officer's attention. The initial prosecution view will be an important factor in the determining officer's assessment and will often be determinative.

63. In cases of dispute the determining officer must decide the status of the material in the light of all the information which is available. The determining officer would be entitled to regard the failure of the parties to reach any agreement, or to seek a ruling from the trial judge, as a powerful indication that the prosecution's initial view as to the status of the material was correct. Otherwise in order to conclude that the material was used the determining officer must be satisfied that the material in question was of central importance to the trial rather than merely helpful to the defence.

64. In the case of R v Ali & Ors (SCCO Ref: 117/17, 153/17, 144/17, 149/17, 10/18,168/17,152/17) it was held that Holroyde J made it clear that it may be entirely appropriate for the prosecution to sever, from a body of electronic data, that which is truly relevant; to exhibit that evidence; and to treat the remainder as unused. It is wrong in principle to treat any form of data which has been reviewed by the prosecution for the purposes of extracting served evidence as though it were used material. Applying Holroyde J's "filing cabinet" analogy, this approach would extend the PPE count not only to the entire content of the filing cabinet, but to the entire content of the office in which it stands. That is not a sustainable approach.

65. Further the Cost Judge commented that that if the status of evidence as unused or served has been raised before a trial judge, as recommended by Holroyde J, then it is incumbent upon any Appellant putting the same issue to a Costs Judge to provide full information about that and to justify raising the issue again. It should not be necessary for the LAA to make its own enquiries. The suggestion that the matter, having been put to the trial judge, should be revisited at a later point before a Costs Judge seems run contrary to Holroyde J's guidance. Further, a Costs Judge would not generally be better placed to determine the issue than the trial judge.

66. It was held in R v Tixe (SCCO Ref 39/19 and 94/19) that simply because it was necessary to consider the material it does not follow that it should be regarded as used material. The normal expectation is that the defence solicitors will consider unused material disclosed by the prosecution.

67. It is not reasonable to assume that because material was not included in an unused schedule or was not accompanied by any covering letter that the material was served as used evidence. As held in R v Jones and Fox (SCCO Ref 182/17) The whole purpose of having the PPE recorded originally and then on NAEs is to demonstrate exactly how much served material there is. If it is not on the NAE, then the assumption is that it is not served. It does not seem to me that it can possibly work the other way around.

68. Where the status of material is uncertain, it is expected that the defence team will agree their position among themselves before claims are submitted to the LAA. It is not possible for material claimed as unused by one team member to also be claimed as PPE by another, and vice versa."

Appendix D also includes a schedule of useful cases relating to PPE. The following extracts relate to cases dealing with unused material in that schedule:

Lord Chancellor v SVS Solicitors [2017] EWHC 1045 (QB)	Unused material may not be paid as PPE. The defence should not be penalised for lack of formal service by the prosecution. Often extracted data can only be fairly considered in light of the surrounding data. Disputes about the status of the material should be resolved by the parties prior to billing, seeking a ruling from the trial judge where necessary. Where the status of the evidence has not been resolved the determining officer must consider all the facts of the case and make a determination. Any view by the prosecution will be an important consideration and in most cases determinative. Where there is any dispute the determining officer must consider whether the material in question was of central importance to the trial. The fact that material was helpful to the defence would not be sufficient for the determining officer to conclude the material was used. Used material may be paid either as PPE or special prep. A qualitative assessment by the determining officer, applying the principles outlined in the Crown Court Fee Guidance is an important and valuable control mechanism which ensures that public funds are not expended inappropriately. Duplicated material should not be included in the PPE.
R v Ali (SCCO Ref 108/16)	That the phone is an exhibit in this case does not mean that data extracted and burned on a disc is evidence in the case. Where the Judge gives a conclusive ruling that the material was unused it is not appropriate for the LAA or the Cost Judge on appeal to go behind that decision. Any ruling by the trial judge should be brought to the LAA's attention when submitting a claim.

R v Ali & Ors (SCCO Ref: 117/17,153/17, 144/17,149/17, 10/18,168/17,152/17)	It is not wrong in principle to treat as unused material any form of data which has been reviewed by the prosecution for the purposes of extracting served evidence. The alternative approach would be to apply Holroyde J's "filing cabinet" analogy, extend the PPE count not only to the entire content of the filing cabinet, but to the entire content of the office in which it stands. That is not a sustainable approach. Holroyde J made it clear that it may be entirely appropriate for the prosecution to sever, from a body of electronic data, that which is truly relevant; to exhibit that evidence; and to treat the remainder as unused.
R v Motaung (SCCO Ref 179/15)	It does not follow that because the schedules prepared by Prosecution and included in the PPE are derived from a larger body of telecommunications data, that the entire body of underlying telecommunications data must also qualify as PPE. This argument blurs the distinction between Pages of Prosecution Evidence, as served upon a defendant, served upon the court and relied upon by the Prosecution, and the wider body of evidence from which it is derived, which may properly be identified as unused material upon which the Prosecution does not rely, but which must be disclosed to a defendant. A single disc may contain both used and unused material.
R v Tixe (SCCO Ref 39/19 and 94/19)	Simply because it was necessary to consider the material it does not follow that it should be regarded as used material. The normal expectation is that the defence solicitors will indeed consider unused material for anything that might assist their client.

Appendix E provides further guidance on claims for viewing unused material. Paragraph 2 reiterates that, *"The LAA can only pay for reasonable time spent considering that material."* Paragraph 7 confirms that generally any disclosed unused material will be payable but also sets out examples of where payment is not made: *"Defence generated material, evidence served in relation to confiscation proceedings and unused material disclosed after the litigator/advocate is no longer representing the client would also not be included, as would other documents not disclosed pursuant to the prosecutors' obligations under CPIA such as title pages, separator pages, index pages, correspondence, etc."*

Paragraph 8 of Appendix E states that, *"It is accepted that both litigators and advocates will need to consider the unused material on behalf of their defendant. However, further information (e.g., word searches, sorting/filtering Excel data etc) as to the approach taken may be requested where large volumes of material are served, especially in electronic format."*

Unfortunately it is not always as clear as it should be what material is evidence as opposed to unused material. Paragraph 9 of Appendix D states: *"Where the status of material is uncertain, each defence team should ensure that they agree their position, and with the court/ CPS where possible, before claims are submitted to the LAA. It should not be possible for a document to be both PPE under the LGFS and unused under the AGFS."*

In judging what is a reasonable amount of time to consider unused material, paragraph 11 of Appendix E provides the following steer: *"Claims should be submitted based on work actually done, but as a guide the LAA would usually allow between thirty seconds (for example documentary exhibits such as images and invoices) and up to two minutes (for example documentary statements, comment interviews, medical records, expert reports, MG6Cs, DMDs) per page for the consideration of unused documentary material. Audio/video material is usually allowed at 1.5 minutes per minute of running time. The determining officer may allow a rate outside these guidelines based on the facts of the case and/or where justification has been provided."* It is important, therefore, to provide as much evidence to back up a claim which is outside of the guidelines demonstrating, for example, exceptional nature of the case or of the unused material. It is important to note when making a claim that, as confirmed in paragraph 12 of Appendix E, time paid for reviewing unused material does not include time spent scheduling it or, *"any other ancillary work"*.

In cases involving large volumes of unused material, paragraph 15 of Appendix E states that, *"the determining officer will start from the presumption that all unused material needs to be read."* Paragraph 15 goes on to list a set of factors which may affect the assessment of reasonableness in relation to the time take to consider the unused material:

> *"a. There is a relatively small proportion of material which is, or is likely to be, of importance to a particular defendant's case.*
>
> *b. There is repetition of material.*
>
> *c. The nature and complexity or otherwise of the material, or significant portions of the material, is such that the determining officer may reasonably expect that a fee earner can read and absorb its contents at a faster rate.*
>
> *d. The determining officer may reasonably expect that a particular defendant's instructions, or the nature of their defence, will assist the team when reading and absorbing the material."*...

Claims for reviewing electronic unused material

Paragraph 18 of Appendix E states that in relation to unused material served electronically, particularly in large volumes, *"the determining officer will consider the overall reasonableness of the time spent as opposed to a rate per page allowance."* Paragraph 19 goes on to state that, *"Where time is claimed for electronic unused material, the files in question must be provided. If the files are under 20 MB and are in pdf, doc, rtf, jpeg, png, tiff, or bmp formats they can be uploaded directly into CCD. LAA staff can be granted access to DCS and Egress, or material may also be uploaded to the Secure File*

Exchange (SFE). Removable media should only be provided if it is not possible to upload the material." Paragraph 20 directs that in order to comply with data protection legislation, any removable media should be provided in an encrypted state.

Paragraph 21 of Appendix E provides the following guidance in relation to unused material which is served in Excel format:

> *"21. Where unused is provided in both PDF and Excel formats, the determining officer will base their assessment on the page count generated by the PDF. This is because PDF is designed to mimic presentation on paper, whereas Excel is not, and can offer different page counts depending upon the way in which the information in that format is managed, used or presented. Additional time may be allowed to cross-reference the Excel material with the PDF."*

Paragraph 22 of Appendix E provides the following advice in relation to claims for reviewing unused mobile phone data:

> *"22. Raw telephone billing data and cell site evidence which is unused would ordinarily be checked using a search function and so time actually spent considering the material may be more appropriate. Unused parts of telephone handset downloads often comprise of large sections of incomprehensible meta data concerning configurations, calendar entries that have no defendant input data, and images sections which comprise preinstalled graphics, logos, flags and emojis that can be quickly discounted. Again, time actually spent considering such material would be more appropriate."*

When approaching the assessment of unused material, paragraph 27 of Appendix E sets out a list of questions that the determining officer may ask when assessing a claim:

> *"a. Has all the necessary supporting documentation been provided?*
>
> *b. When was the material disclosed?*

c. Can the material in question be physically viewed by the determining officer (sometimes discs are blank, or the contents corrupted), and if password protected have the correct passwords been supplied?

d. What was the defendant charged with?

e. What was the defendants' specific role (conspiracy cases)?

f. What is the origin of the data and who is it attributable to e.g., defendant, co-defendant, complainant, third party etc?

g. What is the material in question e.g., telephone download, call data, financial information etc?

h. What format is it in?

i. Does the electronic material contain a large number of blank pages or sections containing no data (e.g., in an Excel document)?

j. Is there any duplication either of electronic material in multiple formats or between material on disc and as uploaded to DCS/served in paper format?

k. Is a search function a more appropriate way of navigating and finding data in electronic material?"

Prosecution fees

In complex cases, a Disclosure Counsel may be instructed, being paid on an agreed hourly rate and granted a specific number of hours per stage of the case. In most cases, however, remuneration to prosecution advocates for reviewing unused material will fall within the graduated fees scheme.

The CPS's 'Graduated Fee Scheme F Manual of Guidance' sets out the principles and details of how the CPS Graduated Fee Scheme F should be applied. Scheme F applies to all hearings, in existing and new cases, that take place on or after 2 May 2023.

Unused material is addressed at paragraph 75, which states:

> *"75. Payment for the consideration of unused material will be paid in one of two ways under Scheme F:*
>
> *"1) Unused material additional fee (UM1)* All elected Cracked Trials and Effective Trial main hearings (incl. retrials) will attract an additional fee (UM1) equivalent to 1½ hours. This will be paid automatically and covers up to 3 hours spent considering the unused material.*
>
> *2) Unused material at the GFS hourly rate – UM2 Reasonable time spent considering unused material, over and above the 3 hours assumed within UM1, will be paid at the GFS hourly rate on production of detailed work records (UM2). Work records must include all work undertaken on the unused, including the first 3 hours covered by UM1"*

Paragraphs 70 and 71 of the CPS Graduated Fee Scheme Guidance covers PII and third-party material:

> *"70. Pages of sensitive unused material considered by the advocate on the instruction of CPS in relation to a PII application will be remunerated by way of time reasonably spent viewing that material upon production of detailed electronic work records…*
>
> *71. Pages of material produced by a third party (for example the Local Authority, Social Services etc.) will not be counted in the page count. Time spent reviewing this material will, however, be remunerated in accordance with the payment arrangements for unused material (UM1 and UM2) as detailed in paragraph 75."*

INDEX

MORE BOOKS BY LAW BRIEF PUBLISHING

'A Practical Guide to Confiscation and Restraint' by Narita Bahra QC, John Carl Townsend, David Winch
'A Practical Guide to the Law of Forests in Scotland' by Philip Buchan
'A Practical Guide to Health and Medical Cases in Immigration Law' by Rebecca Chapman & Miranda Butler
'A Practical Guide to Bad Character Evidence for Criminal Practitioners by Aparna Rao
'A Practical Guide to Extradition Law post-Brexit' by Myles Grandison et al
'A Practical Guide to Hoarding and Mental Health for Housing Lawyers' by Rachel Coyle
'A Practical Guide to Psychiatric Claims in Personal Injury – 2nd Edition' by Liam Ryan
'Stephens on Contractual Indemnities' by Richard Stephens
'A Practical Guide to the EU Succession Regulation' by Richard Frimston
'A Practical Guide to Solicitor and Client Costs – 2nd Edition' by Robin Dunne
'Constructive Dismissal – Practice Pointers and Principles' by Benjimin Burgher
'A Practical Guide to Religion and Belief Discrimination Claims in the Workplace' by Kashif Ali
'A Practical Guide to the Law of Medical Treatment Decisions' by Ben Troke
'Fundamental Dishonesty and QOCS in Personal Injury Proceedings: Law and Practice' by Jake Rowley
'A Practical Guide to the Law in Relation to School Exclusions' by Charlotte Hadfield & Alice de Coverley
'A Practical Guide to Divorce for the Silver Separators' by Karin Walker
'The Right to be Forgotten – The Law and Practical Issues' by Melissa Stock
'A Practical Guide to Planning Law and Rights of Way in National Parks, the Broads and AONBs' by James Maurici QC, James Neill et al
'A Practical Guide to Election Law' by Tom Tabori
'A Practical Guide to the Law in Relation to Surrogacy' by Andrew Powell
'A Practical Guide to Claims Arising from Fatal Accidents – 2nd Edition' by James Patience
'A Practical Guide to the Ownership of Employee Inventions – From Entitlement to Compensation' by James Tumbridge & Ashley Roughton
'A Practical Guide to Asbestos Claims' by Jonathan Owen & Gareth McAloon

'A Practical Guide to Stamp Duty Land Tax in England and Northern Ireland' by Suzanne O'Hara
'A Practical Guide to the Law of Farming Partnerships' by Philip Whitcomb
'Covid-19, Homeworking and the Law – The Essential Guide to Employment and GDPR Issues' by Forbes Solicitors
'Covid-19 and Criminal Law – The Essential Guide' by Ramya Nagesh
'Covid-19 and Family Law in England and Wales – The Essential Guide' by Safda Mahmood
'A Practical Guide to the Law of Unlawful Eviction and Harassment – 2nd Edition' by Stephanie Lovegrove
'Covid-19, Brexit and the Law of Commercial Leases – The Essential Guide' by Mark Shelton
'A Practical Guide to Costs in Personal Injury Claims – 2nd Edition' by Matthew Hoe
'A Practical Guide to the General Data Protection Regulation (GDPR) – 2nd Edition' by Keith Markham
'Ellis on Credit Hire – Sixth Edition' by Aidan Ellis & Tim Kevan
'A Practical Guide to Working with Litigants in Person and McKenzie Friends in Family Cases' by Stuart Barlow
'Protecting Unregistered Brands: A Practical Guide to the Law of Passing Off' by Lorna Brazell
'A Practical Guide to Secondary Liability and Joint Enterprise Post-Jogee' by Joanne Cecil & James Mehigan
'A Practical Guide to the Pre-Action RTA Claims Protocol for Personal Injury Lawyers' by Antonia Ford
'A Practical Guide to Neighbour Disputes and the Law' by Alexander Walsh
'A Practical Guide to Forfeiture of Leases' by Mark Shelton
'A Practical Guide to Coercive Control for Legal Practitioners and Victims' by Rachel Horman
'A Practical Guide to the Law of Driverless Cars – Second Edition' by Alex Glassbrook, Emma Northey & Scarlett Milligan
'A Practical Guide to TOLATA Claims' by Greg Williams
'A Practical Guide to Elderly Law – 2nd Edition' by Justin Patten
'A Practical Guide to Responding to Housing Disrepair and Unfitness Claims' by Iain Wightwick

'A Practical Guide to the Law of Bullying and Harassment in the Workplace' by Philip Hyland
'How to Be a Freelance Solicitor: A Practical Guide to the SRA-Regulated Freelance Solicitor Model' by Paul Bennett
'A Practical Guide to Prison Injury Claims' by Malcolm Johnson
'A Practical Guide to the Small Claims Track – 2nd Edition' by Dominic Bright
'A Practical Guide to Advising Clients at the Police Station' by Colin Stephen McKeown-Beaumont
'A Practical Guide to Antisocial Behaviour Injunctions' by Iain Wightwick
'Practical Mediation: A Guide for Mediators, Advocates, Advisers, Lawyers, and Students in Civil, Commercial, Business, Property, Workplace, and Employment Cases' by Jonathan Dingle with John Sephton
'The Mini-Pupillage Workbook' by David Boyle
'A Practical Guide to Crofting Law' by Brian Inkster
'A Practical Guide to the Law of Domain Names and Cybersquatting' by Andrew Clemson
'A Practical Guide to the Law of Gender Pay Gap Reporting' by Harini Iyengar
'NHS Whistleblowing and the Law' by Joseph England
'Employment Law and the Gig Economy' by Nigel Mackay & Annie Powell
'A Practical Guide to Noise Induced Hearing Loss (NIHL) Claims' by Andrew Mckie, Ian Skeate, Gareth McAloon
'An Introduction to Beauty Negligence Claims – A Practical Guide for the Personal Injury Practitioner' by Greg Almond
'Intercompany Agreements for Transfer Pricing Compliance' by Paul Sutton
'Zen and the Art of Mediation' by Martin Plowman
'A Practical Guide to the SRA Principles, Individual and Law Firm Codes of Conduct 2019 – What Every Law Firm Needs to Know' by Paul Bennett
'A Practical Guide to Adoption for Family Lawyers' by Graham Pegg
'A Practical Guide to Industrial Disease Claims' by Andrew Mckie & Ian Skeate
'A Practical Guide to Redundancy' by Philip Hyland
'A Practical Guide to Vicarious Liability' by Mariel Irvine
'A Practical Guide to Applications for Landlord's Consent and Variation of Leases' by Mark Shelton
'A Practical Guide to Relief from Sanctions Post-Mitchell and Denton' by Peter Causton

'A Practical Guide to Equity Release for Advisors' by Paul Sams
'A Practical Guide to Financial Services Claims' by Chris Hegarty
'The Law of Houses in Multiple Occupation: A Practical Guide to HMO Proceedings' by Julian Hunt
'Occupiers, Highways and Defective Premises Claims: A Practical Guide Post-Jackson – 2nd Edition' by Andrew Mckie
'A Practical Guide to Financial Ombudsman Service Claims' by Adam Temple & Robert Scrivenor
'A Practical Guide to Running Housing Disrepair and Cavity Wall Claims: 2nd Edition' by Andrew Mckie & Ian Skeate
'A Practical Guide to Holiday Sickness Claims – 2nd Edition' by Andrew Mckie & Ian Skeate
'Arguments and Tactics for Personal Injury and Clinical Negligence Claims' by Dorian Williams
'A Practical Guide to Drone Law' by Rufus Ballaster, Andrew Firman, Eleanor Clot
'A Practical Guide to Compliance for Personal Injury Firms Working With Claims Management Companies' by Paul Bennett
'RTA Allegations of Fraud in a Post-Jackson Era: The Handbook – 2nd Edition' by Andrew Mckie
'RTA Personal Injury Claims: A Practical Guide Post-Jackson' by Andrew Mckie
'On Experts: CPR35 for Lawyers and Experts' by David Boyle
'An Introduction to Personal Injury Law' by David Boyle

These books and more are available to order online direct from the publisher at www.lawbriefpublishing.com, where you can also read free sample chapters. For any queries, contact us on 0844 587 2383 or mail@lawbriefpublishing.com.

Our books are also usually in stock at www.amazon.co.uk with free next day delivery for Prime members, and at good legal bookshops such as Wildy & Sons.

We are regularly launching new books in our series of practical day-to-day practitioners' guides. Visit our website and join our free newsletter to be kept informed and to receive special offers, free chapters, etc.

You can also follow us on Twitter at www.twitter.com/lawbriefpub.

www.ingramcontent.com/pod-product-compliance
Lightning Source LLC
LaVergne TN
LVHW052253200926
848481LV00002B/354
* 9 7 8 1 9 1 6 6 9 8 1 9 2 *